CONTENTS

INTRODUCTION

There can be few skills whose acquisition gives as much pleasure as sugarcraft, not only to the student but also to the friends and family members who enjoy the fruits of his or her labours. First attempts at crafts such as pottery or sewing usually end up hidden away at the back of cupboards; with sugarcraft the evidence is eaten - and nobody minds if the initial efforts are less than perfect!

*This book has been designed as a simple introduction to the craft. It opens with a description of equipment required (very little) and a guide to preparing cake tins (pans). Basic recipes for sponge cakes and a Madeira are given, with step-by-step photographs and instructions that ensure perfect results every time. Fruit cakes have not been included, since their preparation - and the marzipanning and royal icing skills they demand - is fully covered elsewhere in the **Sugarcraft Skills** Series.*

Most of the ingredients used are readily available in local supermarkets. To ensure peak flavour, always choose good quality ingredients, particularly in regard to fats and chocolate.

Suggestions are given throughout the book for flavourings. By all means experiment with new combinations, but remember that flavours and colours often develop in cooking and on standing, so it is always wise to err on the side of caution.

All the basic cakes may be made in advance and stored in the freezer; Madeira cakes and American sponges improve if made a day or two in advance. Whisked sponges are best eaten within 48 hours.

The secret of a good moist cake is to split the sponge into thin layers, brushing each layer with warm glaze before assembling with the chosen filling. In addition to recipes for simple glazes, fillings and toppings, there are fully illustrated recipes for creams, buttercreams, fudge icings, frostings and pouring icings. Buttercream paste, a marvellous icing which can be rolled like marzipan or moulded like sugarpaste, is also included, and there's a valuable beginner's guide to chocolate work.

Some of the icings are simple and swiftly made, while others take a little more time and may involve the technique of sugar boiling. Step-by-step illustrations take the mystique out of this process, and simple visual tests are included for those who do not yet own a sugar thermometer. With the exception of frosted fresh flowers, edible cake decorations are used. These range from simple chocolate curls to runout and piped designs. Some bought decorations, such as crystallised violets are included.

The second part of the book has no fewer than eighteen designs for cakes, from a simple daisy that a child would enjoy making to an exquisite cake decorated with frosted fresh flowers that would be perfect for grandmother's birthday. There are sophisticated gâteaux, special occasion cakes for christenings and Christmas, and imaginative novelty items like the vegetable-filled trug illustrated on page 59.

New techniques are introduced gradually, always with illustrations, so that even an outright novice will soon build up an impressive range of skills.

Storage instructions for cakes as good as these are generally superfluous, since they have a tendency to disappear swiftly. Remember, however, that cakes should be assembled a few hours before serving to allow the flavours to develop. Choose a cool place for storage - the refrigerator if the cake contains cream; a dry spot if covered with a frosting that needs to remain crisp.

EQUIPMENT

Little is needed by way of special equipment to make the cakes in this book. Most of the items listed below will be found in the average kitchen, although you may wish to invest in a few more icing tubes (tips), a sugar (candy) thermometer and a serrated plastic scraper. It is a good idea to reserve a sieve, rolling pin and a couple of new wooden spoons exclusively for baking and decorating.

CAKE TINS (PANS) Most of the simple cakes in this book are cooked in two shallow tins rather than one deep tin. Choose rigid tins with straight sides, and measure across the bottom.

BOWLS Large glass or china bowls are best for mixing. Since they are heatproof they can be placed over hot water and can be thoroughly cleaned; essential when whisking egg whites.

SPOONS Use measuring spoons for accurate measuring of small amounts. A large metal spoon is essential for folding in dry ingredients. Wooden spoons are used for beating and creaming mixtures, and for stirring ingredients in a saucepan.

KNIVES A small sharp knife is useful for cutting round templates on buttercream paste or marzipan. Use a large palette knife for spreading icing over the top of cakes, and a small one for coating the sides. For cutting cakes, a serrated knife is most successful.

WHISKS/MIXERS Use a metal balloon whisk for whipping cream or whisking egg whites. These allow the maximum amount of air to be incorporated while leaving a hand free for adding other ingredients. Electric mixers are useful, particularly for one-stage cakes.

SIEVES A fine metal sieve should be kept exclusively for sifting dry ingredients. Soft fruits may be pressed through a nylon or plastic sieve.

PAPER/CARD Tracing paper and thin card are required for templates. Use greaseproof or non-stick paper (parchment) for lining tins (pans) and good quality parchment for making piping bags.

PIPING TUBES (TIPS) Much of the piping in this book is done using a plain piping bag, snipped at the end. However, a writing tube, small star tube, basket tube and leaf tube would be useful.

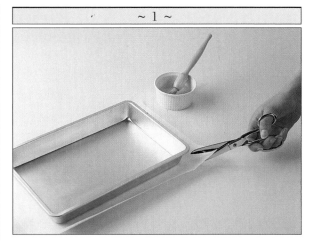

~ 1 ~

SQUARE, RECTANGULAR AND SWISS ROLL TINS (JELLY ROLL PANS) *Place tin on a piece of greaseproof paper (parchment) and draw around the base. Cut around the shape, leaving a 5cm (2 in) margin all round for a deep tin; a 2.5cm (1 in) margin for a shallow tin. Cut diagonally in from corners to marked line.*

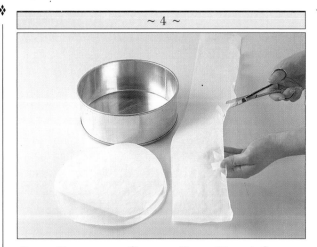

~ 4 ~

DEEP ROUND AND SQUARE TINS (PANS) *Cut two circles/squares to fit base. Cut a piece of paper long enough to go around the tin and 5cm (2 in) deeper. (For square tins cut the paper in two lengths; allow extra for overlapping.) Make a 2.5cm (1 in) fold along length of paper; snip at intervals between edge of paper and fold.*

~ 2 ~

Brush base and sides of tin (pan) with melted vegetable fat (shortening), place paper in tin and brush it into position so that it lies flat against the sides. The cut paper at the corners should overlap. Brush paper lightly with vegetable fat and dust with flour, see step 3.

~ 3 ~

ROUND TINS (PANS) Shallow tins are base lined only. Place tin on paper, draw around base and cut out circle. Brush melted vegetable fat (shortening) over base and sides of tin and position paper circle. Brush with fat. Sprinkle a little flour into tin. Knock sides of tin against your hand to coat evenly; tip out excess flour.

~ 5 ~

Brush side and base of tin (pan) with melted vegetable fat (shortening). Place one of the prepared circles/squares on base. Brush prepared paper strip(s) into position around side of tin, with snipped edge lying flat on base. (For square tins, join paper at sides.) Put in second circle/square of paper; brush with melted fat.

~ 6 ~

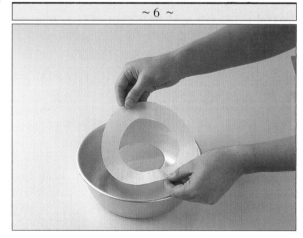

RING TIN (TUBE PAN) Draw around base of tin as though there were no hole in the middle. Cut out circle, fold in half and cut out hole slightly larger than the centre of the tin. Brush tin with melted vegetable fat (shortening). Fit paper into base of tin. It should lie flat when brushed with melted fat.

VICTORIA SANDWICH CAKE

❖

Preheat oven, prepare tins (pans), following instructions on pages 6-7, and set out ingredients, with chosen flavouring. Follow the step-by-step instructions opposite. The quantities below are suitable for two 20cm (8 in) round layers or an 18cm (7 in) square cake. For two 23cm (9 in) layers or a 20cm (8 in) square cake, increase quantity of butter to 250g (8 oz), caster (superfine) sugar to 250g (8 oz/1 cup), eggs to 4 and flour to 250g (8 oz/2 cups).

185g (6 oz) butter, softened
185g (6 oz/¾ cup) caster (superfine) sugar
3 eggs, beaten
185g (6 oz/1½ cups) self-raising flour

FLAVOURINGS

Chocolate Substitute 30g (1 oz/¼ cup) flour with cocoa (unsweetened cocoa powder).
Coffee Add 3 tsp instant coffee with flour.
Citrus Add finely grated rind of 1 lemon.lime or orange before adding eggs.

QUICK MIX SPONGE

The mixture is suitable for a 20 x 30cm (8x12 in) rectangular cake or two 23cm (9 in) round cakes. Flavour as above.

250g (8 oz) soft margarine
250g (8 oz/1 cup) caster (superfine) sugar
4 eggs, beaten
250g (8 oz/2 cups) self-raising flour
1½ tsp baking powder
2 tbsp hot water

Preheat oven to 180°C (350°F/Gas 4). Prepare tins, pages 6-7. Beat ingredients for 2-3 minutes with an electric mixer until light and fluffy. Spoon into tin and bake for 25-30 minutes, until golden and firm to touch.

~ 1 ~

Preheat oven to 190°C (375°F/Gas 5). Beat softened butter and sugar together in a bowl, using either a wooden spoon or an electric mixer. When ready, mixture will be pale in colour and light and fluffy in consistency. Grated citrus rind may be added at this stage.

~ 4 ~

Scrape mixture into prepared cake tins (pans). Spread out evenly. Level surface of mixture with the back of a metal spoon, taking care not to pack the mixture down too firmly.

~ 2 ~

Add a little egg at a time, beating hard between each addition, until mixture has slackened, then add remaining egg a little more quickly. If eggs are cold or added too quickly, the mixture may curdle. If this happens, add 1-2 tbsp flour to stabilize mixture.

~ 3 ~

Sift half the flour into the bowl with coffee or cocoa, if using. Fold gently into mixture, using a large metal spoon. Cut through to the bottom of the bowl employing a figure-of-eight action. Repeat with remaining flour. Do not overmix, but stop when all flour has been incorporated.

~ 5 ~

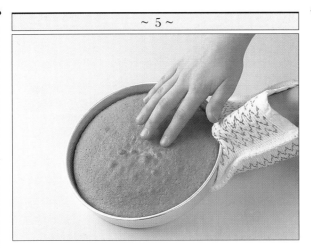

Place cake tins (pans) on a shelf just above the centre of the oven. Check that tins do not touch each other or the sides of the oven. Bake 3-egg mixture for 20-25 minutes; 4-egg mixture for 25-30 minutes. When cooked, cakes will be golden in colour and the top will spring back when gently pressed.

~ 6 ~

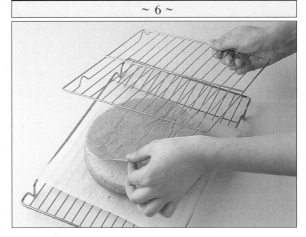

Put a piece of greaseproof paper (parchment) on top of the cake and invert a wire rack on top. Turn cake out onto rack, carefully peel off lining paper and then replace it lightly. Using a second rack, repeat the process to turn the cake the right way up. Remove top paper; and leave the cake to cool. Repeat with second cake.

GENOESE SPONGE

❖

The recipes on this page are both for whisked sponges. Properly prepared, they are beautifully light, but should be eaten within two days of being baked. Before preparing mixture, preheat oven, prepare tins (pans), following instructions on pages 6-7, and set out ingredients. Follow the step-by-step method opposite. The quantities below are for two 20cm (8 in) round layers or an 18cm (7 in) square cake. For two 23cm (9 in) layers or a 20cm (8 in) square cake, increase caster (superfine) sugar to 185g (6 oz/¾ cup), eggs to 6, plain (all-purpose) flour to 185g (6 oz/1½ cups) and butter to 90g (3 oz).

125g (4 oz/½ cup) caster (superfine) sugar
4 eggs
125g (4 oz/1 cup) plain (all-purpose) flour
flavourings, see Swiss Roll (Jelly Roll),
below
50g (2 oz) butter, melted

SWISS ROLL

❖

Swiss (jelly) rolls can be prepared in next to no time. In advance, preheat oven, prepare tin (pan), following the instructions on pages 6-7, and set out ingredients. Follow the step-by-step method opposite. The quantities below are suitable for a 20 x 30cm (8 x 12 in) Swiss roll tin (jelly roll pan).

90g (3oz/⅓ cup) caster (superfine) sugar
3 eggs
90g (3oz/¾ cup) plain (all-purpose) flour
½ tsp baking powder
flavourings, see below

FLAVOURINGS

CHOCOLATE Substitute 15g (½ oz/2 tbsp) flour with cocoa (unsweetened cocoa powder).
COFFEE Add 2 tsp instant coffee with flour.
NUT Fold in 1 tbsp finely ground nuts with flour.

~ 1 ~

GENOESE *Preheat oven to 180°C (350°F/Gas 4). Combine sugar and eggs in a heatproof bowl. Whisk over hot water until mixture is very thick, pale and creamy. When whisk is lifted, its trail should be visible on the surface of the mixture for a few seconds. Remove bowl from heat and continue whisking for 3-5 minutes more.*

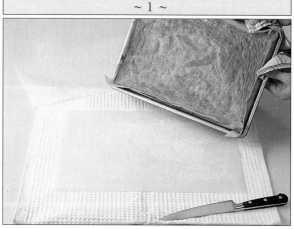

~ 1 ~

SWISS ROLL *Preheat oven to 220°C (425°F/Gas 7). Prepare mixture as above; sifting baking powder with flour. Omit butter. Bake for 7-8 minutes, until firm. Spread out a clean, damp tea-towel. Top with greaseproof paper (parchment) dusted with caster (superfine) sugar. Have ready filling, or second sheet of paper.*

~ 2 ~

Sift flour and any dry flavourings onto a sheet of greaseproof paper (parchment). Sift again over the surface of the mixture. Drizzle the warm butter around the edge of the bowl. Gently fold in, using a figure-of-eight movement to ensure that all flour has been incorporated. Take care not to overbeat or mixture will deflate.

~ 3 ~

Divide mixture between prepared tins (pans), gently tapping the sides against your hand to level the mixture into the corners. Try to avoid using a knife or spoon to spread the mixture. Bake at once. A 4-egg mixture will require 15-20 minutes; a 6-egg mixture 20-25 minutes.

~ 2 ~

Invert cooked sponge onto sugared paper and carefully peel off lining paper. Trim edges all around cake. To assist in rolling, make a shallow cut along one short side of the cake. If using a filling such as jam or fruit butter, warm gently and spread over warm cake. Alternatively, place second sheet of paper on top of sponge.

~ 3 ~

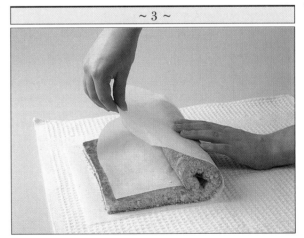

Fold sponge on cut line and roll up, with filling or paper inside. Use sugared paper underneath cake as a guide. Hold rolled sponge in position for a few seconds with join underneath. Peel cake off sugared paper; cool on wire rack. When cold, unroll, remove inner paper and spread with cream, fudge filling or buttercream. Re-roll.

AMERICAN SPONGE

❖

This is a firm white sponge which is a good base for novelty cakes or petits fours, see page 28. In advance, preheat oven, prepare tin (pan), following instructions on pages 6-7, and set out ingredients. Follow the step-by-step method opposite. The quantities below are suitable for a 20cm (8 in) round or 18cm (7 in) square cake. Double all quantities for a 23cm (9 in) round or a 20cm (8 in) square cake.

125g (4 oz) butter
185g (6 oz/¾ cup) caster (superfine) sugar
½ tsp vanilla essence (extract)
220g (7 oz/1¾ cups) plain (all-purpose) flour
2 tsp baking powder
125ml (4 fl oz/½ cup) water
4 egg whites

MADEIRA CAKE

❖

A traditional cake with a firm texture. Follow the step-by-step method opposite. The quantities below are suitable for a 20cm (8 in) round or an 18cm (7 in) square cake. For a 23cm (9 in) or shallow 25cm (10 in) round or a 20cm (8 in) square cake, increase butter to 315g (10 oz), caster (superfine) sugar to 315g (10 oz/1¼ cups), eggs to 6, self-raising flour to 280g (9 oz/2¼ cups) and plain (all-purpose) flour to 125g (4 oz/1 cup).

250g (8 oz) butter, softened
250g (8 oz/1 cup) caster (superfine) sugar
grated rind and juice of 1 lemon
5 eggs, beaten
220g (7 oz/1¾ cups) self-raising flour
90g (3 oz/¾ cup) plain (all-purpose) flour

~ 1 ~

AMERICAN SPONGE *Preheat oven to 180°C (350°F/ Gas 4). Beat butter, caster (superfine) sugar and vanilla together in a bowl until light and fluffy, using either a wooden spoon or an electric mixer. Vanilla sugar may be used instead of caster sugar, in which case omit the essence (extract).*

~ 1 ~

MADEIRA *Preheat oven to 160°C (325°F/Gas 3). In a warm bowl, cream butter and sugar with lemon rind, using either a wooden spoon or an electric mixer. When ready, mixture will be pale in colour and light and fluffy in consistency. Gradually add eggs, beating well between each addition. Add a little flour, if necessary, to prevent curdling.*

~ 2 ~

Sift flour and baking powder together. Add to creamed mixture alternately with water, beating well between each addition, until smooth. Break down any lumps of flour immediately by pressing them against the side of the bowl. In a clean, dry, grease-free bowl, whisk egg whites until stiff but not dry.

~ 3 ~

Add egg whites to cake mixture a little at a time, folding them in with a clean metal spoon. Use a figure-of-eight action, taking care not to overmix. Scrape mixture into cake tin (pan). Bake 4-egg white mixture for 35-45 minutes; 8-egg white mixture for 55-65 minutes. Remove from tin (pan), following Step 6, page 9.

~ 2 ~

Sift flours together into a bowl. Sift again into the creamed mixture, adding about one third at a time and folding in carefully with a large metal spoon. Cut through to the bottom of the bowl with a figure-of-eight action. Add sufficient lemon juice to make a soft dropping consistency. If more liquid is needed, add water or milk.

~ 3 ~

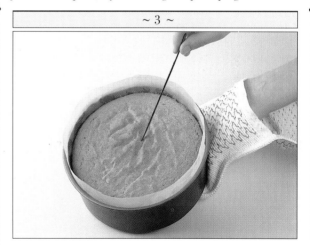

Scrape mixture into tin (pan). Bake 5-egg mixture for 1½-1¾ hours; 6-egg mixture for 1¾ - 2 hours, covering cake with greaseproof paper (parchment) after about 1 hour to prevent overbrowning. When cooked, a warm skewer inserted into the cake should come out clean. Cool in tin, then invert onto a wire rack.

FILLINGS,
TOPPINGS & FLAVOURINGS

The basic cakes on pages 8-13 can be transformed by the addition of glazes, fruit syrups, fresh cream, custard and fruit fillings.

APRICOT GLAZE

Use to seal cut surfaces or brush over cakes before coating in marzipan or pouring fondant.

250g (8 oz/1 cup) apricot jam
2 tbsp lemon juice

Warm jam in a small saucepan until melted. Press through a sieve into a clean pan and stir in lemon juice. Boil for 30 seconds, then remove from heat. Cool slightly, then apply to cake with a clean brush. Makes about 250ml (8 fl oz/1 cup).

VARIATIONS

BLACKCURRANT GLAZE A dark glaze is more appropriate for chocolate cakes. Follow recipe above, but substitute blackcurrant or strawberry jam or cranberry jelly for apricot jam.

MARMALADE GLAZE As above, but substitute orange, lime or ginger marmalade for jam.

FRUIT SYRUP

Fruit syrup adds flavour, colour and moisture to a cake and may be used as a topping

125ml (4 fl oz/½ cup) fresh fruit juice,
chopped soft fruit or fruit purée
125ml (4 fl oz/½ cup) Sugar Syrup, page 24

Mix ingredients in a small saucepan. Place over low heat and beat until thoroughly combined. If chopped fruit has been used, purée in a blender or food processor. If necessary, rub mixture through a sieve to remove any seeds. Makes 250ml (8 fl oz/1 cup).

FRUIT BUTTER

Make fruit butter when apples and soft fruits are plentiful. The rich pulp makes a flavoursome addition to a cream filling. Refrigerate.

250g (8 oz) cooking apples, peeled and
chopped
185g (6 oz) soft fruits such as blackcurrants or
raspberries
155ml (¼ pt/⅔ cup) apple juice
60g (2 oz/¼ cup) caster (superfine) sugar
grated rind and juice of 1 orange

Combine apples, soft fruit and apple juice in a small heavy-bottomed saucepan. Cook over low heat until fruit is soft. Stir in sugar, orange rind and juice. Continue to cook over low heat until a thick pulp is formed. Makes about 500g (1 lb).

FRESH CREAM

WHIPPED CREAM is popular as a cake filling and may also be piped as a simple topping. For whipping, use equal quantities of fresh single (light) and double (heavy) cream. Chill bowl, whisk and cream in advance. Whip mixture until it stands in soft peaks, adding any liquid flavouring, right. Take care not to overwhip; the cream will stiffen on standing. Nuts or fruit purées should be folded in, using a metal spoon, after cream has been whipped. Cakes filled or decorated with cream should be kept refrigerated.

PIPING Add 1 tbsp milk, single (light) cream or plain yogurt to every 155ml (¼ pt/⅔ cup) double (heavy) cream. Chill bowl, whisk and cream, then whip mixture to soft peaks. Pipe as for buttercream. Piped cream will keep its shape for up to 48 hours and may be frozen for up to 4 weeks.

CHANTILLY CREAM

❖

250ml (8 fl oz/1 cup) double (heavy) cream
30g (1 oz/2 tbsp) icing (confectioners') sugar
few drops of vanilla essence (extract)

Whip cream lightly in a bowl. Sift in icing (confectioners') sugar and vanilla. Whip again until soft peaks form. Sufficient to fill and thinly coat an 18cm (7 in) layer cake.

CHOCOLATE GANACHE

❖

A wonderfully rich mixture which whips to double its volume when chilled. Add liqueur with caution; too much may curdle the ganache.

250g (8 oz/8 squares) dark dessert chocolate
(German dark chocolate), chopped
250ml (8 fl oz/1 cup) double (heavy) cream
½ -1 tsp liqueur

Mix chocolate and cream in a heavy-bottomed saucepan. Melt chocolate over low heat, stirring constantly with a wooden spoon. Still stirring, heat for 10 minutes or until smooth and thick. Do not boil. Pour into a clean bowl, cool, then refrigerate for 1 hour. Stir in liqueur. Whisk until ganache is pale in colour and has doubled in volume. Sufficient to fill and coat an 18cm (7 in) layer cake.

CITRUS CHEESE CREAM

❖

125g (4 oz/⅔ cup) full fat cream cheese
60g (2 oz/¼ cup) caster (superfine) sugar
grated rind of ½ lemon
3 tbsp lemon juice
6 tbsp whipped cream

Cream cheese and sugar together in a bowl. Gradually beat in lemon rind and juice, then fold in cream. Sufficient to fill and coat an 18cm (7 in) layer cake.

FLAVOURING FOR ICINGS & FILLINGS

❖

ALMOND For the best flavour, use roasted almonds, finely chopped or ground. If using almond essence (extract) add sparingly or the flavour will dominate. See also Praline, page 30.
CHESTNUT Unsweetened chestnut purée may be mixed with caster (superfine) sugar, butter and rum to make a traditional filling for a Yule log. The chestnut purée may also be mixed with whipped cream.
CHOCOLATE Add melted or finely chopped dark or bitter dessert chocolate (German dark chocolate).
CITRUS The finely grated rind and juice of oranges, lemons and limes gives icings and cream fillings colour, flavour and texture. Scrub fruit with a fine brush under hot water to remove preserving wax. Dry with absorbent kitchen paper, then grate finely, using a clean pastry brush to extract all the rind from the grater. Strain juice and add it sparingly, remembering that flavours will develop further on standing.
COFFEE Chill freshly filtered strong black coffee. Add 1-2 tbsp or to taste.
GINGER A little finely chopped stem (preserved) ginger makes a delicious addition to whipped cream. The syrup from the jar may be added, too, but use it sparingly.
LIQUEUR Tia Maria, Amaretto, Chartreuse, Cointreau, Curaçao, Kirsch, Maraschino, Grand Marnier, Crème de Cassis, Crème de Menthe and coffee-flavoured liqueurs are all suitable for flavouring (and in some cases, colouring). Rum and brandy may be used sparingly.
MOCHA Use a combination of chocolate and coffee; the coffee flavour should dominate.
RASPBERRY/STRAWBERRY Use fresh fruit with whipped cream, or make into syrup or fruit butters, see left.

CREME PATISSIERE

❖

Custards, stabilized with flour or cornflour (cornstarch) make good cake fillings. To make the crème pâtissière follow the step-by-step method opposite. All recipes on this page yield about 315ml (½ pt/1¼ cups).

315ml (½ pt/1¼ cups) milk
1 vanilla pod (bean)
2 egg yolks
60g (2 oz/¼ cup) caster (superfine) sugar
30g (1 oz/¼ cup) plain (all-purpose) flour
few drops of vanilla essence (extract) or
30g (1 oz) grated chocolate, optional

CREME DIPLOMATE

3 tsp custard powder or 4 tsp cornflour
(cornstarch)
1 tbsp caster (superfine) sugar
155ml (¼ pt/ ⅔ cup) milk
155ml (¼ pt/ ⅔ cup) double (heavy) cream
few drops of vanilla essence (extract)

Blend custard powder or cornflour (cornstarch) and sugar with a little milk in a saucepan. Stir in remaining milk and cook over moderate heat, stirring constantly, until thick and smooth. Pour into a bowl, cover and chill. Whip cream until thick and fold into chilled custard with vanilla.

FRUIT MOUSSE FILLING

❖

Follow the step-by-step method opposite.

155ml (¼ pt/⅔ cup) fruit purée or juice
1 tsp powdered gelatine
1 quantity Quick Meringue Frosting,
see page 24
155 ml (¼ pt/⅔ cup) double (heavy) cream

~ 1 ~

CREME PATISSIERE *Heat milk with vanilla pod (bean) to boiling point; remove from heat. Combine egg yolks and sugar in a bowl and beat vigorously for several minutes until light in colour and thick and creamy in texture. Sift in flour and beat well until mixture is smooth.*

~ 1 ~

FRUIT MOUSSE FILLING *Put half the fruit purée or juice in a small saucepan and sprinkle gelatine over the surface. Leave to soften for 2-3 minutes until sponged. Stand saucepan over a gentle heat and stir gelatine until dissolved. Stir in remaining purée or juice, remove from heat and allow to cool.*

~ 2 ~

Remove vanilla pod (bean) and pour warm milk in a steady stream onto egg mixture, stirring constantly until smooth. Return mixture to clean saucepan and bring to the boil over moderate heat. Lower the heat and simmer, stirring, for 2-3 minutes more until smooth and thick. Stir in grated chocolate, if using.

~ 3 ~

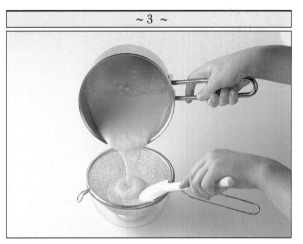

To ensure that Crème Pâtissière is smooth and velvety, press mixture through a sieve into a clean bowl. If vanilla pod (bean) was not used to flavour milk, stir in vanilla or other liquid flavouring. Cover surface of crème lightly with damp greaseproof paper (parchment) to prevent formation of a skin. Chill before use.

~ 2 ~

Fold 2 tbsp of the cool fruit mixture into the meringue frosting, using a metal spoon or whisk and a figure-of-eight action. Gradually add remaining fruit mixture in the same way until all has been incorporated and the meringue frosting is evenly coloured.

~ 3 ~

Whip cream to soft peaks, see page 14, and fold gently into mousse mixture, using the same method as in step 2. Do not add cream too quickly or filling may collapse. If this happens, chill mixture thoroughly, then whip again. Keep filling chilled before and after use.

*O*ne of the delights of sugarcraft is finding out how even the simplest icings and techniques can be utilised to produce exciting and interesting cakes. Decoration is as much about imagination as it is about ingredients, and a simple design in buttercream can be highly effective. It would be a shame to stop there, though, when there are numerous other icings, frostings and toppings to try.

BASIC BUTTERCREAM

❖

A simple butter icing which may be made in advance. The only drawback with buttercream is that its natural colour makes some tints difficult to achieve. If a specific colour is required, use American Parfait, see page 22. Follow the step-by-step method opposite. Sufficient to fill and coat a 20cm (8 in) layer cake.

185g (6 oz) butter, softened
2 tbsp milk or fruit juice
375g (12 oz/2¼ cups) icing (confectioners')
sugar
flavouring, see page 15
food colouring, optional

CREME AU BEURRE

❖❖

The basis of this rich icing is a sugar syrup which is added to beaten egg yolks before being combined with butter. Make sure that the eggs are perfectly fresh and all utensils spotlessly clean. Follow the step-by-step method opposite. The quantity below will cover a 20cm (8 in) cake.

90g (3 oz/ ⅓ cup) caster (superfine) sugar
4 tbsp water
2 egg yolks
185g (6 oz) unsalted butter, softened
flavouring, see page 15

~ 1 ~

BASIC BUTTERCREAM *Place softened butter in a large bowl. Gradually add milk or fruit juice, working the mixture together until creamy. For a less rich icing, a soft butter and vegetable spread may be used, in which case less liquid will be required. Grated citrus rind or liquid flavouring may be added at this stage.*

~ 1 ~

CREME AU BEURRE *Make a syrup, using caster (superfine) sugar and water, and following method described for sugar syrup in steps 1 and 2 on pages 24-25. Using a balloon whisk, whisk egg yolks in a bowl until pale in colour. Pour in syrup in a thin, steady stream. Continue to whisk until all the syrup has been incorporated and the mixture is thick and creamy.*

~ 2 ~

Sift in icing (confectioners') sugar with any dry flavouring such as cocoa. Gradually stir in sugar, then beat hard with a wooden spoon or electric mixer until pale, light and fluffy. A little extra liquid may be needed if a soft icing is required.

~ 3 ~

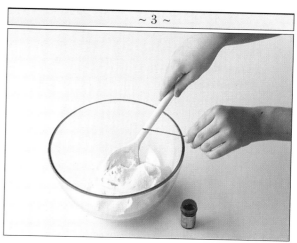

A little food colouring may be added during the final beating. Pale colours may be altered slightly by the butter content of the icing; if colour is crucial, substitute white vegetable fat (shortening), see American Parfait, page 22. If chopped glacé (candied) fruits or nuts are added, fold them in at the end with a metal spoon.

~ 2 ~

Beat softened butter in a separate bowl until light and fluffy. Gradually beat in syrup and egg mixture.

~ 3 ~

Fold or beat in flavourings, as desired. Above shows lemon juice and honey being added to the crème au beurre, as for Honey & Lemon Ring, see page 32.

BUTTERCREAM PASTE

❖

This versatile icing can be rolled out like marzipan and used to cover the top of a cake, making a dry, flat surface for piping and decorating. If a white fat (shortening) is used, it can be subtly tinted for special occasion cakes and the trimmings can be moulded to make flowers. It may be made in advance and briefly stored but should not be refrigerated. Follow the step-by-step method opposite. Makes about 750g (1½ lb).

60g (2 oz) butter or white vegetable fat
(shortening)
2 tbsp lemon juice
2 tbsp water
625-750g (1¼ - 1½ lb/3¼ - 4½ cups) icing
(confectioners') sugar
food colouring and flavouring, see page 15

EXPERT ADVICE

≈

Wrap buttercream paste in greaseproof paper (parchment), then place in a polythene bag. If paste becomes too dry to handle, sprinkle surface with cooled boiled water and leave well wrapped for several hours. Knead well before use.

CHOCOLATE FUDGE ICING

❖

Swirls of this delicious icing turn a Victoria Sandwich Cake into a special treat. Have the cake filled and glazed before making the icing, which sets quickly. A white chocolate version of this icing is on page 22. Follow step-by-step method opposite. Sufficient to cover a 20cm (8 in) cake.

125g (4 oz/4 squares) dark dessert chocolate
(German dark chocolate), broken up
60g (2 oz) butter
1 egg
185g (6oz/1¼ cups) icing (confectioners')
sugar

~ 1 ~

BUTTERCREAM PASTE *Melt fat with lemon juice and measured water in a saucepan over low heat. Stir in 185g (6 oz/1¼ cups) of the icing (confectioners') sugar. Continue to heat, stirring occasionally, for 2-3 minutes or until a few bubbles begin to rise to the surface of the mixture. Do not allow mixture to boil.*

~ 1 ~

CHOCOLATE FUDGE ICING *Combine chocolate and butter in a large heatproof bowl. Set bowl over a saucepan of hot water and leave until chocolate and butter have melted. Alternatively, place bowl in microwave oven on Medium power for 1-2 minutes. The chocolate will soften while retaining its shape; stir into the melted butter.*

~ 2 ~

Stir in a further 185g (6 oz/1¼ cups) icing (confectioners') sugar. Remove from heat and pour mixture into a bowl. Cool slightly, then gradually beat enough of the remaining sugar to make a soft pliable paste. Beat in colouring and/or flavouring, if used.

~ 3 ~

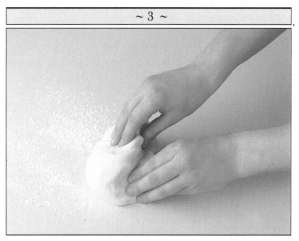

Knead paste in the bowl for a few moments, then transfer to a clean surface which has been lightly dusted with icing (confectioners') sugar. Knead paste until smooth and elastic. The longer the paste is kneaded, the lighter it will become. If not using at once, wrap thoroughly (see Expert Advice, left).

~ 2 ~

Cool chocolate mixture slightly, then beat in egg, using a wooden spoon. Beat vigorously for about 30 seconds, then stir in icing (confectioners') sugar. Beat mixture until it begins to thicken. When ready, it should coat the back of the spoon.

~ 3 ~

Pour icing quickly over glazed cake, smoothing it with a warmed knife. Alternatively, continue beating until the icing forms soft peaks. Swirl it quickly over glazed cake with a small palette knife, using small circular movements that create soft peaks when the knife is lifted.

VARIATIONS ON BUTTER ICINGS

AMERICAN PARFAIT

American Parfait is preferable to buttercream for coloured icings, since the vegetable fat (shortening) has no definite colour of its own.

185g (6 oz) white vegetable fat (shortening),
softened
2 tbsp milk
375g (12 oz/2¼ cups) icing (confectioners')
sugar
flavouring, see page 15
food colouring

Make icing following step-by-step instructions for Basic Buttercream on pages 18-19. Add colouring sparingly. Sufficient to fill and coat a 20cm (8 in) cake.

MERINGUE BUTTERCREAM

125g (4 oz) butter, softened
1 quantity Quick Meringue Frosting,
see page 24

Beat butter until pale and creamy. Gradually add meringue mixture, beating until smooth and fluffy. Sufficient to cover a 20cm (8 in) cake.

WHITE CHOCOLATE FUDGE ICING

Have the cake ready before starting to make this icing. The method is similar to that used for Chocolate Fudge Icing on pages 20-21.

125g (4 oz/4 squares) white chocolate
60g (2 oz) butter
185g (6oz/1¼ cups) icing (confectioners')
sugar
1-2 tbsp milk

Melt chocolate in a heatproof bowl set over a saucepan of hot water. Melt butter in a small saucepan. Let both ingredients cool slightly, then mix them together and beat vigorously for about 30 seconds. Stir in icing (confectioners') sugar, with 1 tbsp milk. Beat mixture until thick enough to coat the back of the spoon, adding remaining milk if necessary. Use at once. Sufficient to coat a 20cm (8 in) cake.

CREAM CHEESE ICING

Not strictly a butter icing this, but made in much the same way. It is rich creamy and without being cloying and is the perfect spread for carrot cake or a citrus-flavoured Madeira.

125g (4 oz/½ cup) full fat cream cheese
60g (2 oz/¼ cup) caster (superfine) sugar
grated rind of ½ lemon
2 tbsp lemon juice
90ml (3 fl oz/⅓ cup) double (heavy) cream,
whipped

Cream the cheese with the sugar in a bowl. Beat in the lemon rind and juice, then fold in the cream. Sufficient to coat a 20cm (8 in) cake.

COOKED ICINGS

Glaze and fill cakes before making these icings, as they set quickly and must be poured over the cakes while still warm if a smooth effect is to be created. For a thicker icing that can be drawn into peaks, continue to beat the icing as it cools.

CARAMEL ICING

❖

4 tbsp caster (superfine) sugar
2 tsp water
90g (3 oz) butter, melted
6 tbsp single (light) cream
375g (12 oz/2¼ cups) icing (confectioners')
sugar, sifted

Put sugar in a small heavy-bottomed saucepan. Add measured water. Stir occasionally over moderate heat until sugar has melted, then boil without stirring until syrup turns pale brown. Immediately add butter and cream, stirring constantly until caramel dissolves. Remove pan from heat and add icing (confectioners') sugar, beating until smooth and creamy. Spread warm icing over cake, smoothing it with a warm dry palette knife. Leave to cool and set before serving. Sufficient to coat a 20cm (8 in) cake.

CHOCOLATE LIQUEUR ICING

❖

125g (4 oz/4 squares) dark dessert chocolate
(German dark chocolate), chopped
125g (4 oz) butter
125g (4 oz/¾ cup) icing (confectioners') sugar
3 tsp orange or coffee liqueur

Melt chocolate, butter and sugar in a saucepan over low heat, stirring occasionally. Do not overheat. Remove from heat and stir in liqueur. Leave icing to cool and thicken slightly before pouring and smoothing over cake. Sufficient to coat a 20cm (8 in) cake.

CREAMY FUDGE ICING

❖

125g (4 oz) butter
125g (4 oz/⅔ cup) soft dark brown sugar
3 tbsp milk
315g (10 oz/2 cups) icing (confectioners')
sugar

Combine butter and brown sugar in a saucepan. Add milk and stir over moderate heat until butter and sugar have melted. Remove from the heat, add icing (confectioners') sugar and beat until cool and thick. Sufficient to coat a filled 23cm (9 in) cake.

ORANGE CREAM ICING

❖

3 egg yolks
125g (4 oz/½ cup) caster (superfine) sugar
1 tsp grated orange rind
4 tbsp orange juice
125ml (4 fl oz/½ cup) double
(heavy) cream

Combine the egg yolks, sugar and orange rind in the top of a double boiler (double saucepan). Beat until mixture is pale and light. Set over simmering water. Gradually add orange juice, beating constantly until mixture thickens. Remove from the heat and set aside until cool. Chill. In a bowl, whip cream until stiff. Fold into orange mixture. Sufficient to coat a 20cm (8 in) cake.

FROSTINGS

*A*lthough the term *frosting* is today loosely applied to a wide range of cake coverings, usually cooked or partly cooked, it originally meant an icing made from egg white and sugar. The sugar is whisked into egg whites over heat or made into a syrup before being poured onto whisked whites. Step-by-step instructions for making a sugar syrup are given opposite.

SUGAR SYRUP

❖

This syrup may be stored in a clean screw-topped jar for several weeks, but will crystallize if refrigerated.

250g (8 oz) granulated sugar
pinch of cream of tartar
4 tbsp water

QUICK MERINGUE FROSTING

185g (6oz/¾ cup) caster (superfine) sugar
1 large egg white
pinch of cream of tartar
Combine ingredients in a greasefree heatproof bowl. Place over a saucepan of simmering water; whisk constantly until mixture thickens and stands in soft peaks. Remove from heat. Whisk until cool. Use immediately. Sufficient to cover an 18cm (7 in) cake.

AMERICAN FROSTING

❖

Firm outside and soft underneath, this meringue icing may be folded into fruit mousses, custard fillings or buttercreams. Follow the step-by-step method opposite. Sufficient to cover a 20cm (8 in) cake.

250g (8 oz/1 cup) granulated sugar
pinch of cream of tartar
4 tbsp water
2 egg whites

~ 1 ~

Sugar Syrup *Place sugar and cream of tartar in a small heavy-bottomed saucepan. Add measured water and stir over moderate heat until sugar has melted. Continue to heat, without stirring, until syrup begins to bubble gently.*

~ 1 ~

American Frosting *Using the sugar, cream of tartar and measured water, make a syrup as described above, continuing to heat the mixture until it registers 115°C/240°F on a sugar (candy) thermometer. Alternatively, test by dropping about ½ tsp syrup into a small bowl of cold water. If you can mould it to a soft ball between your fingers, the syrup is ready,*

~ 2 ~

Boil without stirring until syrup measures 105°C/ 220°F on a sugar (candy) thermometer. Alternatively, test by dipping a teaspoon in the syrup and then pressing another teaspoon onto the back of it. Gently separate the spoons. If a fine thread forms, the syrup is ready.

~ 3 ~

Remove pan from heat immediately and plunge the bottom of it into ice cold water. This will arrest the cooking process and prevent syrup from caramelizing. When cool, pour syrup into a clean warm glass jar with a screw top. If syrup thickens on standing, warm it gently by standing jar in a bowl of warm water.

~ 2 ~

Whisk egg whites in a clean, greasefree bowl until very stiff. Holding the pan of syrup high above the bowl, pour it in carefully in a steady stream, constantly whisking the mixture with a balloon whisk until all the syrup has been incorporated.

~ 3 ~

Whisk in any flavouring or colouring, then continue to whisk mixture until soft peaks form when the whisk is lifted. Quickly spread frosting over prepared cake, drawing it into peaks or swirls with a warm dry palette knife.

POURING ICINGS

GLACE ICING

❖

As its name suggests, this resembles a glaze. It has limited application, as it cannot be piped or swirled, and sets quickly. However, it is very useful as a quick topping for a simple family cake or batch of cupcakes. A common fault when making glacé icing is to add too much liquid too soon. At first the icing will be stiff, but it will soon slacken as the liquid is absorbed by the icing (confectioners') sugar. When ready, the icing should be slack enough to find its own level.

185g (6 oz/1¼ cups) icing (confectioners')
sugar
2-3 tsp warm water
flavouring and/or colouring as desired

Sift icing (confectioners') sugar into a bowl and gradually add liquid, stirring constantly until icing slackens sufficiently to coat the back of the spoon. Orange or lemon juice may be used instead of water, but if a chocolate icing is required it is preferable to add butter or oil as in the recipe below. Pour icing over cake, smoothing surface with a spatula which has been dipped in hot water. Apply any decorations quickly, avoiding any that might shed colour. Sufficient to top a 20cm (8 in) cake.

CHOCOLATE GLAZE

❖

185g (6 oz/6 squares) dark dessert chocolate
(German dark chocolate), chopped
2 tsp vegetable oil
60g (2 oz/¼ cup) caster (superfine) sugar
4 tbsp boiling water

Combine ingredients in a heatproof bowl. Place over hot (not boiling) water and stir until chocolate has melted. Remove from heat and stir occasionally until icing begins to thicken. Pour slowly over cake. Sufficient to top a 20cm (8 in) cake.

FONDANT

❖

There is a great deal of confusion about fondant, largely because the term was at one time applied to sugarpaste and other moulding icings. Fondant is a pouring icing, traditionally used on petits fours, which has at its base a white paste that should be made in advance and diluted with syrup when required. Step-by-step instructions for making the basic fondant mixture are given opposite, while the recipe for Petits Fours on page 28 clearly illustrates its use.

500g (1 lb/2 cups) caster (superfine) sugar
3 tsp liquid glucose or pinch of cream of tartar
6 tbsp water

EXPERT ADVICE

≈

Make fondant at least 24 hours before it is required, so that paste can mature. When preparing fondant it is important to keep the sides of the pan free of sugar crystals. A dampened pastry brush is ideal for this purpose. Allow plenty of time for working and kneading paste. Store in a tightly covered jar in a cool place (not the refrigerator) for up to two months.

Before fondant can be used, it must be melted over gentle heat. Avoid overheating, which could spoil the glossy appearance. Sugar syrup is frequently added to create the correct consistency for pouring. At this stage a few drops of colouring may be added, or flavouring provided in the form of essential oils such as peppermint oil (available from health food shops). Use very sparingly - a single drop may be sufficient. Cool melted chocolate may also be stirred into the liquid fondant. Some specialist cake decorating shops sell fondant, either in its paste form or as a powder to be dissolved with water or syrup.

~ 1 ~

FONDANT *Make a syrup, using caster (superfine) sugar, glucose or cream of tartar and measured water. Follow the method described in step 1, page 24. When syrup registers 115°C/240°F, the soft ball stage, pour it onto a wetted marble slab or cool greasefree surface and allow it to cool slightly.*

~ 2 ~

Using two scrapers or spatulas, scrape the syrup from the sides to the centre, using a figure-of-eight movement. Continue working the fondant in this fashion for about 5 minutes or until it forms a stiff white paste.

~ 3 ~

Break off pieces of fondant and knead firmly until smooth and supple. Finally knead all the small pieces together to form a ball. Place in a clean bowl, cover with a damp clean cloth and leave for 24 hours to mature before storing in a screw-topped jar for up to 2 months. Do not store in the refrigerator.

~ 4 ~

To prepare a pouring fondant icing, place fondant in a clean bowl over a saucepan of hot (not boiling) water. Stir occasionally until melted. Add 1 tbsp sugar syrup. Continue to heat mixture, adding more syrup if necessary, until it coats the back of the spoon. Add colouring and flavouring as desired.

PETITS FOURS

*T*hese iced shapes provide the perfect opportunity for practising new skills. They may be filled with any of the butter icings on pages 18-22 or with fresh cream.

4-egg white American Sponge mixture,
see page 12

FILLING AND COATING

½ quantity Basic Buttercream, see page 18
Apricot Glaze, see page 14
double quantity Fondant, see page 26
Sugar Syrup, see page 24
¼ tsp instant coffee dissolved in ½ tsp hot
water
additional flavourings and colourings as
desired

DECORATION

use any or all of the following: marzipan
(almond paste), glacé (candied) cherries,
blanched almonds, stem (preserved) ginger,
crystallized rose petals or violets, chocolate
motifs, see page 44

Preheat the oven to 180°C (350°F/Gas 4). Bake the cake in a lined and greased 20cm (8 in) square cake tin (pan). Cool on a wire rack.

Warm fondant, disolving it with sugar syrup to the consistency of thick cream, see page 27. Flavour some of the fondant icing with the coffee and tint or flavour the rest as desired. Cut up, ice and decorate the cakes, following the step-by-step instructions right. When fondant has set, trim the base of each cake neatly with a sharp knife.

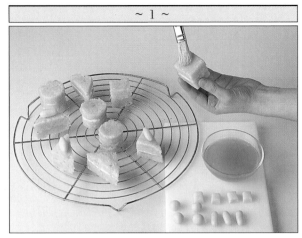

~ 1 ~

Cut cake in half horizontally, brushing off any loose crumbs. Spread cut halves with buttercream and sandwich back together again. Cut into neat rounds, squares or triangles, again brushing away loose crumbs. Coat with apricot glaze. A marzipan roll, nut or half glacé (candied) cherry may be placed on top of each cake, if liked.

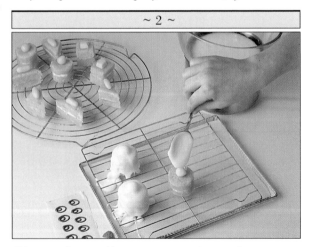

~ 2 ~

Place cakes well apart on a wire rack over wax paper. Pour fondant icing slowly from a large spoon over the top of each cake, letting it trickle slowly down the sides. If free from crumbs, fondant that falls through onto the paper may be scraped up and used again. Decorate with nuts, ginger, crystallized rose petals or chocolate motifs.

ALMOND MERINGUE GATEAU

*M*eringue, praline and crème pâtissière turn a simple sponge into a special cake.

3-egg Victoria Sandwich Cake mixture,
see page 8
1 egg white
60g (2 oz/¼ cup) caster (superfine) sugar
60g (2 oz/½ cup) ground almonds
almond essence (extract) to taste
FILLING AND COATING
125ml (4 fl oz/½ cup) double (heavy) cream
1 quantity chilled Crème Pâtissière,
see page 16
almond essence (extract) to taste
PRALINE
185g (6 oz/1½ cups) whole blanched almonds
185g (6 oz/¾ cup) caster (superfine) sugar

● Preheat oven to 190°C (375°F/Gas 5). Divide cake mixture between two lined and greased 20cm (8 in) round cake tins (pans).

● Whisk egg white in a clean, greasefree bowl until stiff, then fold in sugar, ground almonds and essence (extract). Spread meringue over cake mixture in one of the tins (pans). Bake plain cake layer for 20-25 minutes; meringue layer for about 5 minutes longer. Remove from tins and cool on a wire rack, with meringue topping uppermost.

● Make praline. Combine almonds and sugar in a small heavy-bottomed saucepan. Stir over low heat until sugar has dissolved and turned a pale caramel colour. Spoon out 20 caramelized almonds and set aside for topping. Tip remaining mixture onto an oiled baking sheet. Set aside to cool, then place in a strong polythene bag and crush with a rolling pin. Tip crushed praline into a sieve set over a bowl. Reserve both sieved and crushed praline.

● In a bowl, whip cream until stiff. Fold into chilled crème pâtissière with the almond essence (extract). Spread one third of the almond-flavoured cream over meringue-topped cake layer. Place plain layer on top. Set aside one third of the remaining cream and use the rest to coat the sides of the cake.

● Chill cake and reserved cream for 30 minutes. Coat side of cake in crushed praline, following instructions below. Spread remaining cream over top of cake, taking care not to disturb praline coating on sides. Arrange reserved caramelized almonds around rim. Mark lines on topping and dust them with the reserved sieved praline as illustrated opposite.

COATING THE SIDE OF THE CAKE *Sprinkle praline (or other coating) thickly along a piece of greaseproof paper (parchment) or foil. Place one hand, palm down, on top of the cake and the other palm up underneath it. Turn the cake and roll it lightly over the praline. Do not press heavily or the sides will be unevenly coated.*

HONEY & LEMON RING

A rich honey and rum glaze soaks into this cake to provide a taste of the unexpected under the buttercream topping.

*4-egg white American Sponge mixture,
see page 12*
T O P P I N G
*2 lemons
4 tbsp clear honey
2 tbsp rum
1 quantity Crème au beurre, see page 18*
L E M O N   S T R A N D S   &   L I M E   T W I S T S
*1 lemon, rind only
1 lime
2 tbsp caster (superfine) sugar*

● Preheat oven to 180°C (350°F/ Gas 4). Bake cake in a lined and greased 1.1 litre (2 pt/5 cup) ring tin (tube pan) for 25-30 minutes.
● Meanwhile make glazed lemon strands and lime twists, following the instructions right.
● Invert cake on a wire rack. Wash and dry the tin (pan) and place a ring of greaseproof paper (parchment) in the base. Return the warm cake to the tin.
● Make topping. Grate one of the lemons and squeeze them both. Set grated rind aside. Reserve 4 tsp of the lemon juice. Pour remaining juice into a small saucepan. Stir in half the honey and all the rum. Heat, without boiling, until honey melts, then pour mixture slowly over cake. Leave to cool in tin (pan). When quite cold, carefully transfer to a serving plate.
● Make crème au beurre. Beat in reserved lemon rind and juice with remaining honey, see step 3, page 19. Spread icing over cake, smoothing it with a small palette knife. Holding the prongs of a fork against the side of the cake, slowly rotate the plate to create a design. Mark the top of the cake in a similar fashion, following illustration opposite. Decorate with the glazed lemon strands. Make a cut in each lime slice from outer edge to centre; twist slices. Add lime twists to cake. If not serving at once, store cake in a cool place. Eat within two days.

LEMON STRANDS AND LIME TWISTS *Cut thinly pared lemon rind into strands. Thinly slice lime. Place in a pan with water to cover; simmer for 5 minutes. Remove strands/slices with slotted spoon. Add sugar to pan; stir until dissolved. Boil, without stirring, until pale brown. Return strands/slices. When caramel coated, remove and spread out on a plate to dry. Twist slices, following instructions above.*

RICH VELVET CROWN CAKE

3-egg Victoria Sandwich Cake mixture,
see page 8
90g (3 oz/3 squares) dark plain (semi-sweet)
chocolate, melted
TOPPING AND DECORATION
60g (2 oz/ 2 squares) cooking chocolate
125g (4 oz/4 squares) white chocolate
Apricot Glaze, warmed, see page 14
1 quantity Chocolate Liqueur Icing (page 23)
2 tsp icing (confectioners') sugar

● Preheat oven to 190°C (375°F/Gas 5). Base line and grease a 1.1 litre (2 pt/5 cup) ring tin (tube pan). Make a paper piping bag, following the step-by-step instructions right. Melt cooking chocolate and half the white chocolate in separate bowls and make chocolate fans, following step-by-step instructions on page 42.

● Divide cake mixture between two bowls and fold the melted dark plain (semi-sweet) chocolate into one of them. Put alternate spoonfuls of plain and chocolate mixture into the tin (pan), occasionally drawing a skewer through the mixture. Bake for 20-25 minutes. Cool on a wire rack, removing lining paper. Leaving the cake on the rack, brush generously all over with apricot glaze.

● Make chocolate icing and pour it slowly round the top of the cake so that it falls down to cover the sides. Smooth any uncovered areas with a palette knife. Transfer cake to a plate when set.

● Melt remaining white chocolate in a bowl over hot water. Stir in icing (confectioners') sugar until dissolved. Spoon mixture into piping bag and snip off the end. Pipe lines up the sides and over the top of the cake. Finish the cake by placing alternate dark and white chocolate fans around the top, as shown opposite.

~ 1 ~

Cut a piece of good quality greaseproof paper (parchment) into a rectangle measuring 25 x 20 cm (10 x 8 in). Cut the paper in half diagonally and place one piece flat on table with small point nearest to you. Fold right-hand point over to centre point, making a cone. Hold in position with thumb and first finger of left hand.

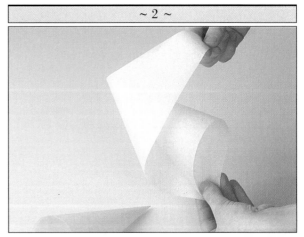

~ 2 ~

Lift the paper off the table. Pick up the final point with the right hand and wrap it over the cone so that all three points meet together underneath. Fold the points over twice to secure the cone. For plain icing, snip off tiny piece straight across the pointed end of the cone. For flowers make a diagonal cut and for leaves cut either side to form a small 'V'.

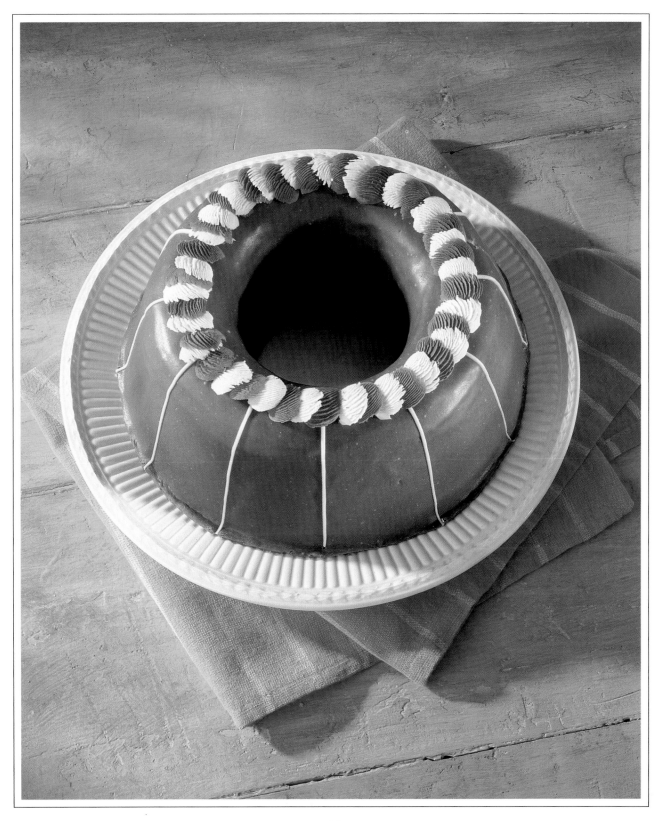

COFFEE & WALNUT GATEAU

*M*eringue frosting, crisp on the outside, creamy underneath, gives this delectable coffee cake a touch of class.

6-egg coffee-flavoured Genoese Sponge mixture, see page 10
10 walnuts to decorate
FILLING AND COATING
250ml (8 fl oz/1 cup) double (heavy) cream
125ml (4 fl oz/½ cup) strong black coffee, chilled
3 tbsp icing (confectioners') sugar
60g (2 oz/½ cup) finely chopped walnuts
double quantity Quick Meringue Frosting, see page 24

● Preheat oven to 180°C (350°F/Gas 4). Bake cake in three lined and greased 20cm (8 in) round cake tins (pans). Cool on a wire rack.
● Make the cream filling, see instructions right. Using half the cream filling for each layer, spread cream over two sponges and sprinkle each with chopped walnuts. Layer cake up with plain sponge on top.
● Place a small circle of wax paper or foil on top of a small upturned plate which has a diameter slightly less than that of the cake. Place cake on top of paper. Put cake in a cool place.
● Make frosting and quickly spread it over top and side of cream-filled cake, see step 3, page 70. When set, carefully slide cake onto a serving plate. Decorate with walnuts. If liked, walnuts may be glazed. Follow the instructions for lemon strands and lime slices on page 32. Keep gâteau in a cool place (not the refrigerator). Serve the same day.

CREAM FILLING *In a bowl, whip cream to soft peaks, then continue whipping while slowly adding coffee in a thin steady stream. Gradually add icing (confectioners') sugar, continuing to whip cream until thick.*

DAISY CAKE

*T*his novel method of presentation means that the cake is already in neat serving portions for your guests.

Quick Mix Sponge mixture, see page 8
ICING AND DECORATION
1 quantity Basic Buttercream, see page 18
1-2 tbsp lemon juice
green, yellow and orange food colouring
125g (4 oz/1⅓ cups) fine desiccated coconut
1 quantity Glacé Icing, see page 26
60g (2 oz) marzipan (almond paste)
mimosa balls, optional
125g (4 oz/4 squares) dark dessert chocolate
(German dark chocolate), chopped

● Preheat oven to 180°C (350°F/Gas 4). Bake cake in a lined and greased 20 x 30cm (8 x 12 in) cake tin (pan). Cool on a wire rack. Make a thin cardboard template of a petal 8.5cm (3½ in) long. Prepare a 56 x 38cm (22 x 15 in) cake board.

● Make up buttercream, slackening it with lemon juice. Colour 2 tbsp of the buttercream green and set it aside. Colour remaining buttercream yellow. Put two thirds of the coconut into a bowl. Add a few drops of yellow food colouring and stir until evenly coloured. Colour remaining coconut orange. Cut out parts for daisy, coat in buttercream and coconut and assemble cake on a board, following step-by-step instructions opposite.

● Make up glacé icing and colour it yellow. Flood top of each petal with glacé icing, using the same technique as for Raspberry Valentine Cake on page 62. Knead green food colouring into marzipan (almond paste). Roll it to a long sausage for the daisy stem. Sprinkle chocolate around daisy as shown in illustration.

~ 1 ~

Cut 10cm (4 in) circle from corner of cake for daisy centre. Using template and sharp knife, cut out 13 petal shapes (12 petals and 1 leaf). Brush away any loose crumbs on the sides of the petal shapes, using a dry pastry brush. Assemble the daisy on the cake board.

~ 2 ~

Spread side and top of daisy centre liberally with buttercream. Roll in orange coconut, using same technique as for praline on page 30. Coat sides of petals only in buttercream, making sure it comes above the top edge; roll in yellow coconut. Colour remaining yellow coconut green. Use with green buttercream to coat leaf.

MOTHERING SUNDAY CAKE

*F*illed with a delicious blackberry mousse and coated with toasted almonds, this special cake is perfect for Mother.

3-egg Victoria Sandwich Cake mixture,
see page 8
FILLING AND DECORATION
1 quantity Fruit Mousse Filling made with
125g (4 oz) fresh blackberries, see page 16
250g (8 oz) marzipan (almond paste)
125g (4 oz/1 cup) slivered almonds
60g (2 oz/2 squares) dark dessert chocolate
(German dark chocolate)
pink, yellow and green food colouring

● Preheat oven to 190°C (375°F/Gas 5). Bake cake in two lined and greased 20cm (8 in) round cake tins (pans). Cool on a wire rack. Make several paper piping bags, following instructions on page 34. Prepare fruit mousse filling and leave to cool.

● Using a long serrated knife, split each cake in half horizontally. Set aside one quarter of the fruit mousse filling and spread the rest over three of the sponge layers. Layer cake up with plain sponge on top. Spread remaining filling around the side and thinly over the top of the cake. Place cake in refrigerator for 30 minutes to set.

● Roll 185g (6 oz) of the marzipan (almond paste) into a 20cm (8 in) round and smooth it over the top of the cake, taking care not to disturb the fruit mousse coating on the side. Protecting your hand in an oven glove, heat a metal skewer in a flame. Press skewer down firmly on marzipan, marking it in a diagonal pattern as shown in illustration. Wipe and re-heat skewer each time a line is marked.

● Toast almonds on a piece of foil under a medium grill, turning frequently until golden brown. Cool. Coat side of cake in toasted almonds, using the same technique as for praline on page 30. Make sure nut coating comes well up at the top edge to hide edge of marzipan (almond paste).

● Cut a 20cm (8 in) circle from greaseproof paper (parchment) and write the word 'Mother' boldly on it. Place on top of cake and pinprick out the word. Melt chocolate and place it in a paper piping bag. Snip off the end and quickly pipe 'Mother' on the cake. Go over inscription again, this time holding bag slightly to the side of the piped line to make the letters thicker. Alternatively, pipe the inscription on wax paper; peel off and transfer to cake when dry.

● Finally, colour remaining marzipan and make small flowers and leaves to arrange on the cake, following the instructions below.

MARZIPAN FLOWERS *Mould a tiny marzipan cone. Pinch one end for stalk; pull out the other between first and second fingers. Snip with scissors to make petals, or use a daisy cutter. Roll tiny ball of marzipan for centre. Pull up petals; leave to set.* ***LEAVES*** *Cut diamond shapes, mark veins; drape over a small rolling pin to dry.*

BLACK FOREST CAKE

A perennial favourite, Black Forest Cake is a chocoholic's dream.

*4-egg chocolate-flavoured Genoese Sponge
mixture, see page 10*
1 quantity Chocolate Ganache, see page 15
*250g (8 oz/¾ cup) whole fruit morello
cherry jam*
2 tbsp lemon juice
2 tbsp maraschino syrup
DECORATION
3 maraschino cherries
125g (4 oz/4 squares) cooking chocolate
60g (2 oz/2 squares) white chocolate
3 small rose leaves

● Preheat oven to 180°C (350°F/Gas 4). Bake cake in two lined and greased 20cm (8 in) round cake tins (pans). Cool on a wire rack.

● Make up Ganache mixture; refrigerate for 1 hour before whisking. Meanwhile make chocolate decorations, following instructions right. Use dark chocolate for scrolls and white chocolate for cherries and leaves.

● Combine jam, lemon juice and maraschino syrup in a saucepan. Stir over low heat until jam has softened. Brush melted jam liberally over both sponge layers to cover, then spoon out cherries remaining in saucepan and spread them over one of the cakes.

● Whisk ganache until pale and doubled in volume. Spread one third of it over the cherries. Place second sponge on top, jam side down. Spread remaining ganache over top and side of cake and smooth over with a palette knife . Press chocolate scrolls around side of cake and arrange half-dipped cherries and leaves on top. Chill cake before serving.

~ 1 ~

Melt chocolate as described on page 44. **CHERRIES** *Drain maraschino cherries and dry on absorbent kitchen paper. Half dip them in warm chocolate. Leave to dry on wax paper.* **LEAVES** *Wash and dry rose leaves. Brush backs with chocolate. Refrigerate, chocolate side up, until set, then carefully peel leaves off chocolate.*

~ 2 ~

SCROLLS *Spread melted chocolate smoothly over marble or clean smooth surface. Leave until dry. Use a long knife with a rigid blade. Hold knife at an angle of 45° to chocolate. Draw it lightly across to cut thin layers that curl into scrolls.* **FANS** *Make as scrolls, but use the end of a round-bladed knife.*

$\mathscr{C}$hocolate adds flavour, colour and a touch of luxury to cakes and gâteaux. Grating or paring a block of chocolate provides an instant decoration, while melted chocolate may be used in numerous ways - for glazes, icings, frostings, motifs or to dip or coat leaves, nuts and fruit as illustrated on page 42.

COCOA (unsweetened cocoa powder) This has a high starch content. When used in baking, it should replace some of the measured flour.

DRINKING CHOCOLATE (sweetened cocoa powder) Milder in flavour than cocoa, this may be used to make a simple icing. Either sift it in with icing (confectioners') sugar or blend to a paste with a little liquid before adding to other ingredients.

CHOCOLATE A blend of cocoa solids and butter, the texture depends on the amount of added fat. It may be plain or milk, with varying amounts of added sugar. Cake decorating shops sell chocolate either as small button drops or in a block which has been tempered, ready for use. Dark dessert chocolate (German dark chocolate) has the best flavour but is less versatile than the softer cooking chocolate. Use dark chocolate for chopping, grating, and, in its melted form, for adding to cake mixtures and icings. Spread thinly, it can be cut into shapes and used as a decoration. Cooking chocolate is ideal for dipping fruits and nuts, making scrolls and runouts. White chocolate does not contain cocoa solids. It has a soft waxy texture and can be melted and coloured for decorations.

CHOCOLATE-FLAVOURED CAKE COVERINGS These have a large proportion of vegetable oil. Their flavour is poor and is not recommended for cake recipes.

MELTING CHOCOLATE

Do not overheat chocolate or it will scorch. It should always be heated gently and for just long enough to melt it. Chop or break up the chocolate, if necessary, and place it in the top of a double boiler (double saucepan) or a heatproof bowl that fits snugly over the top of a saucepan. Place over hot (not boiling) water, stirring until chocolate melts. Chocolate can be melted in a microwave oven, but care must be taken not to overheat. Consult your handbook for instructions. When heated in the microwave, the chocolate will retain its shape and should be tested with a fork. It cannot be kept warm; any chocolate not used at once must be melted again.

PIPING

Working with small quantities of melted chocolate is difficult, because it sets so quickly. For simple runouts or one-word inscriptions it may be sufficient to place the chocolate in a paper piping bag (page 34), but to keep it fluid longer, stir in a little sugar syrup or icing (confectioners') sugar. For piping lines, see Rich Velvet Crown Cake, page 34.

WORDS AND NUMBERS Put the melted chocolate into the piping bag and test it on a board. It should be fluid enough to flow but thick enough to hold its shape between the top of the bag and the cake, so that it can be directed. If it rushes out, let it cool for a few seconds, then try again.

RUNOUTS Trace the design before melting the chocolate. Pipe around the outer edge of the shape, wait a few seconds until it begins to set, then fill in between the lines by squeezing the bag and working the top from side to side (see page 58).

SHELLS Have ready several piping bags and tubes (tips) as you will need to keep using fresh chocolate. The set chocolate may be returned to the bowl or pan for melting again. Pipe as for buttercream.

MOTIFS To make chocolate motifs, make several tracings of a suitable shape on wax paper. Turn paper over and pipe over visible lines. Leave chocolate to set.

STORING

Store chocolate decorations and chocolate-coated cakes in a cool dry atmosphere. They should be eaten within one week.

Noah's Ark, see page 46

NOAH'S ARK

Illustrated on previous page

*T*his cake would be ideal for a child's birthday. Pipe his or her name on the roof of the cabin in chocolate, if liked. Having made the cake, follow the step-by-step instructions opposite for assembly and decoration. The shapes for the marzipan animals can easily be adapted.

---

*Double quantity Quick Mix Sponge mixture,
see page 8*
ICING
*Blackcurrant Glaze, see page 14
2 quantities Chocolate Fudge Icing,
see page 20
Glacé Icing, see page 26, made using 250g
(8 oz/2¼ cups icing (confectioners') sugar*
DECORATION
*315g (10 oz) white marzipan (almond paste)
125g (4 oz/4 squares) white chocolate
2 ice cream wafers
yellow, pink, brown and blue food colouring*

● Preheat oven to 180°C (350°F/Gas 4). Bake cake in a lined and greased 20 x 30cm (8 x 12 in) cake tin (pan). Cool on a wire rack. Cut up cake, reassemble on a board and decorate as explained opposite.
● When ark is complete, make up a small quantity of glacé icing. Set aside about 2 tbsp of the icing and colour the rest blue. Spread the blue icing around the base of the ark to represent the sea and brush on a little white icing for the wave crests. If liked, add detail to marzipan animals, using buttercream or melted chocolate.

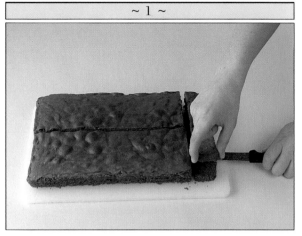

~ 1 ~

Have ready warm blackcurrant glaze and one quantity fudge icing. Cut a 4cm (1½ in) strip from one short side of cake. Split strip in half horizontally, then assemble pieces side by side for ark base, using glaze and icing. Cut remaining piece of cake in half lengthwise, sandwich with glaze and icing and attach to base to make ark.

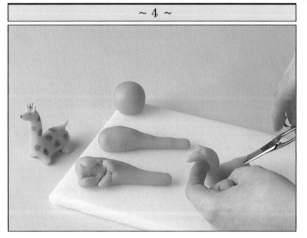

~ 4 ~

GIRAFFES *Colour 60g (2 oz) marzipan (almond paste) pale yellow; cut in half to make two animals. Roll each piece to a thick body with a 5cm (2 in) long neck. With small scissors, snip four legs and mould into shape. Snip a tail. Mould face and snip two ears. Place giraffes on deck, supporting necks over cabin roof. Using food colouring, paint on brown spots.*

~ 2 ~

Trim front and back of ark, cutting at an angle from top piece to base. Stick trimmings together to form cabin base. Trim either side. Set aside. Using 125g (4 oz) marzipan (almond paste), roll out two 25cm (10 in) sausage shapes. Brush top edge of the ark with glaze and position marzipan around edge. Hold in position for a few seconds.

~ 3 ~

Make up second quantity of fudge icing, spread over sides of ark and marzipan; mark to represent wood. Coat cabin base in fudge icing; set aside. Melt white chocolate; brush over one side of each wafer. Pour remaining white chocolate on cake to form deck, brushing up to marzipan. Fix cabin base to cake and stick on wafers for roof.

~ 5 ~

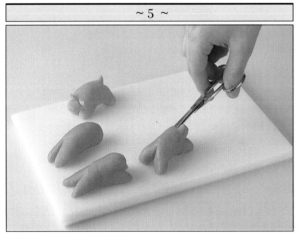

PIGS *Colour 60g (2 oz) marzipan (almond paste) pink; cut in half to make two animals. Roll each piece to a short fat 5cm (2 in) roll with one end fatter than the other. Curve roll in an arch and snip up narrow end to make back legs. Snip up snout from top of other end; cut two front legs from lower section. Mould snout, snip ears and tail. Position on ark.*

~ 6 ~

SQUIRRELS *Colour 60g (2 oz) marzipan (almond paste) brown; cut in half. Cut each half into three pieces, decreasing in size. Roll largest piece into a 5cm (2 in) body; cut up both ends for feet and hands. Sit body upright. Roll smallest piece into head, snip ears; attach with melted chocolate. Shape tail, mark with scissors; stick behind body. Position on ark.*

EASTER NEST

*S*imnel cakes are traditionally made for Easter. This Madeira cake is less rich, but still has the layer of marzipan (almond paste).

5-egg Madeira Cake mixture, see page 12
almond essence (extract) to taste
125g (4 oz) marzipan (almond paste)
icing (confectioners') sugar for rolling out
DECORATION
Apricot Glaze, warmed, see page 14
375g (12 oz) marzipan (almond paste)
125g (4 oz/4 squares) cooking chocolate

Preheat oven to 160°C (325°F/Gas 3). Grease and line a deep 20cm (8 in) round cake tin (pan). Add almond essence (extract) to cake mixture, then place half the mixture in the prepared tin (pan).

On a clean surface dusted with icing (confectioners') sugar, roll out marzipan (almond paste) to a 20cm (8 in) round. Place on top of cake mixture in tin (pan). Carefully smooth remaining mixture over the top.

Bake cake, covering top with greaseproof paper (parchment) if it begins to overbrown. When testing with a skewer, remember that centre will remain soft. Cool slightly before turning out on a wire rack.

When cold, brush top and sides of cake liberally with apricot glaze. Marzipan side of cake in two strips: Measure around cake with a piece of string and cut to size. Measure depth of cake in the same way, adding on 1cm (½ in) before cutting string.

Using 250g (8 oz) of the marzipan, roll out two sausages, each half the length of the longer piece of string. Roll and trim each sausage shape to a strip slightly taller than the cake, using smaller length of string as a guide. Press the fine side of

a grater firmly onto both marzipan strips to make a pattern. Holding cake on its side, roll it along one marzipan strip to fix it firmly in position. Repeat with second strip. Smooth the joins carefully with a small palette knife, taking care not to spoil pattern on marzipan.

Roll out 60g (2 oz) of remaining marzipan into two thin sausage strips, each the same length as the longer piece of string. Twist strips together to form a rope for the top edge of the cake. Fix it in position.

Melt most of the chocolate (reserving a little for piping the eyes of the chicks) and make small scrolls as described on page 42. When dry, sprinkle these over the top of the cake as shown opposite. Use remaining marzipan to make two Easter chicks as described below.

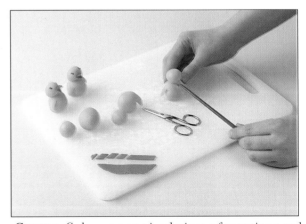

CHICKS *Colour a pea-sized piece of marzipan red and the remainder yellow. Cut the yellow piece in half to make two chicks. Roll a small ball for each head and a larger ball for each body. Assemble the chicks, then make a snip on either side of each chick for the wings. Cut two red diamond shapes for the beaks and insert into the heads. Pipe chocolate eyes.*

DART BOARD

6-egg Madeira Cake mixture, see page 12
COATING AND DECORATION
double quantity
American Parfait, see page 22
90g (3 oz/3 squares) dark dessert chocolate
(German dark chocolate), finely grated
2 tbsp cocoa (unsweetened cocoa powder),
dissolved in 2 tsp boiling water
red and green food colouring

Preheat the oven to 160°C (325°F/Gas 3). Bake the cake in a lined and greased 25cm (10 in) cake tin (pan) for 1½-1¾ hours, if necessary covering the surface with greaseproof paper (parchment) to prevent overbrowning. Cool on a wire rack. Make several paper piping bags, see page 34, fitting one with a medium writing tube (tip).

To ensure a flat surface, turn the cake upside down for icing. Spread the side of the cake with parfait, making sure that it comes well up the sides to what will be the top of the cake. Coat the side of the cake in grated chocolate, using the same technique as for praline, page 30. Reserve some grated chocolate for the outer rim of the dartboard.

Spread parfait thinly over the top of the cake. Spoon 6 tbsp of the remaining parfait into a small bowl and stir in the liquid cocoa. Colour 2 tbsp of the parfait red and a similar quantity green. Place the brown, red and green parfait in separate paper piping bags, spooning the remaining white parfait into the bag fitted with writing tube (tip).

Pipe the design on the cake, as opposite. Cut a 20cm (8 in) circle from wax paper or thin card. Fold it into four. Using a protractor, mark each quadrant into five equal sections. Unfold the paper/card and centre it on the cake. Pipe a line of white icing all around it, with a small dot to mark the boundary of each of the 20 marked sections. Remove the paper/card.

Mark the inner rings by centering a 12.5cm (5 in) paper circle on the cake and piping around it.

The second ring can be piped freehand and the two smaller rings in the centre marked with the wide end of a piping tube (tip) or bottle lid before being piped. Pipe the long unbroken lines radiating out from the centre, following the instructions below. Carefully place the remaining grated chocolate around the outer rim of the cake, up to the white line.

Snip the point off the bag of brown icing and fill in the appropriate spaces by moving the bag backwards and forwards. Using the same method, fill in the remaining sections of the dart board, using the appropriate colours. Finally pipe over the white lines again, starting with the circles and finishing with the straight lines radiating out from the centre.

Finally, pipe the numbers around the edge of the board, cutting off the icing with a knife if it proves difficult to lift off the chocolate.

PIPING THE WHITE LINES *Hold bag at an angle of 45° with tube (tip) on cake. Squeeze bag, at the same time raising tube and move bag towards you, forming a thread of icing. Continue to squeeze and move bag, keeping tube 2.5cm (1 in) above cake so thread falls where required. To finish line, stop squeezing, press tube onto cake and lift up.*

SURPRISE PARCEL

*T*his colourful gift-wrapped parcel cake is not all that it seems. When cut, it reveals a hidden compartment in which a gift or package of sweets may be concealed.

Quick Mix Cake mixture, see page 8
ICING AND DECORATION
1 quantity basic Buttercream, see page 18
juice of ½ lemon
Apricot Glaze, see page 14
wrapped sweets
double quantity Buttercream Paste, see page 20
food colouring

Preheat oven to 180°C (350°F/Gas 4). Bake cake in a lined and greased 20 x 30cm (8 x 12 in) cake tin (pan). Cool on a wire rack. Make the buttercream, slackening it with the lemon juice.

Cut up, glaze and assemble cake as shown in step 1 opposite, using two thirds of the buttercream. Trim sides of cake if necessary to create a neat box shape. Measure sides and top of cake accurately and make a thin cardboard template for each piece. Having made templates, spread top and sides of cake with remaining buttercream, smoothing it with a warm, dry palette knife.

The 'wrapping paper' is made from buttercream paste. The panels for sides of cake and lid are made separately and then assembled. Colour one eighth of the buttercream paste lilac and the rest a pale turquoise. Make panels, following instructions in step 2 opposite. Assemble them around the cake, box-fashion, smoothing joins to seal them neatly.

Use remaining paste to make a contrasting label. Mark edges with a crimper or fork, leave to dry, then paint inscription, using a fine paintbrush and food colouring. When dry, position on cake. Add a length of ribbon, as shown in illustration opposite, if liked.

~ 1 ~

Cut cake across width to make three equal pieces. Place two pieces on top of each other and cut a central 5 x 10cm (2 x 4 in) hole through both. Brush layers with glaze. Using buttercream, sandwich layers with holes on cake board. Place sweets in hole. Spread cake with buttercream; top with plain layer. Set for 30 minutes.

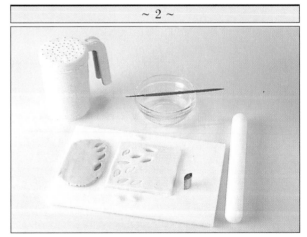

~ 2 ~

Keeping remaining paste tightly covered, roll out a piece of turquoise paste 5mm (¼ in) thick. Using template, cut an end panel. Roll out a small piece of lilac paste to the same thickness. Using an aspic cutter, cut shapes from both pieces. Dampen cut edges round holes in turquoise paste and insert lilac shapes. Seal with fingertips. Make remaining panels.

MUSIC BAR

*T*o celebrate a music student's birthday, this cake is ideal for afternoon tea.

Quick Mix Sponge mixture, see page 8
ICING
quantity Basic Buttercream, see page 18
2 tbsp orange juice
double quantity White Chocolate Fudge Icing,
see page 22
milk (see method)
DECORATION
125g (4 oz/4 squares) dark dessert chocolate
(German dark chocolate)
2 tsp Sugar Syrup, see page 24
60g (2 oz/2 squares) white chocolate
powdered food colourings

● Preheat oven to 180°C (350°F/Gas 4). Bake cake in a lined and greased 20 x 30cm (8 x 12 in) cake tin (pan). Cool on a wire rack. Prepare a 35cm (14 in) long cake board. Make several paper piping bags, following instructions on page 34.

● Make up buttercream stirring in orange juice. Slice cake in half horizontally. Sandwich back together, using one third of buttercream. Cut cake in half lengthwise, and sandwich one layer on top of the other with half the remaining buttercream.

● Leave cake to set for 30 minutes, then trim sides neatly. Spread remaining buttercream in a thin layer over the cake and around the sides.

● Make up fudge icing, adding a little milk to make a smooth, spreading consistency. Spoon icing on top of cake and spread quickly over the top and down the sides to cover. Using a warm, dry palette knife, smooth the icing.

● Trace 3 large and 20 small clefs opposite and make two or three copies of each on the same piece of paper. Secure each tracing to a flat surface with a smooth piece of wax paper on top, see step 2, page 58.

● Using a clean ruler, mark position of lines on cake by pricking surface with a pin. Melt dark chocolate in a small bowl over hot (not boiling) water. Stir in sugar syrup. When chocolate starts to thicken, quickly place 2 tbsp in a piping bag and snip off the end.

● Replace bowl with remaining chocolate over warm water. Pipe lines on cake, following pin-pricks, then pipe round and fill in large clef symbols on wax paper. Leave to set.

● Pipe notes on lines, using fresh chocolate and a fresh bag. Work fast, before chocolate sets in bag. Place remaining chocolate in a fresh piping bag, this time fitted with a small star tube (tip). Pipe small shells around base of cake.

● Melt white chocolate, divide in half and colour in contrasting pastel shades. Fill paper piping bags and pipe around small clefs on paper, each time starting at the bottom of the symbol. Make at least 10 small clefs in each colour.

● When set, carefully peel the best large clef off the paper and stick in position on bar lines. Peel off 16 small clefs and position on sides of cake.

GRANDMA'S
80TH BIRTHDAY CAKE

*F*rosted fresh flowers are perfect for a special celebration. Choose flowers with thin petals such as violets, primroses and sweet peas. The flowers should be frosted the day before to allow time for drying. Inedible flowers should be removed before cutting the cake.

*4-egg Victoria Sandwich Cake mixture,
see page 8*
FILLING AND TOPPING
*2 quantities Meringue Buttercream, see page
22 and Expert Advice right
4 pieces stem (preserved) ginger, finely
chopped
1 quantity Buttercream Paste, see page 20
icing (confectioners') sugar for rolling out
60g (2 oz/2 squares) white chocolate
food colouring to match flowers*
FROSTED FLOWERS
*fresh flowers
egg white, beaten
caster (superfine) sugar*

● Preheat oven to 190°C (375°F/Gas 5). Bake cake in two lined and greased 23cm (9 in) round cake tins (pans). Cool on a wire rack. Split each cake in half horizontally. Place all the layers cut side up. Make several paper piping bags, following instructions on page 34.
● Make up one quantity of meringue buttercream and divide it between three of the cut layers. Sprinkle chopped ginger on top of each. Layer cake up with plain sponge on top, place on a plate and leave to set for 30 minutes.
● Make up buttercream paste. Knead it until smooth, then place in a polythene bag. Make up second quantity of meringue buttercream. Spread a thin layer on the top of the cake. On a surface lightly dusted with icing (confectioners') sugar, roll out buttercream paste to a 23cm (9 in) round.

Run a knife under the round to loosen it, slide both hands underneath and lift it onto top of cake.
● Spread remaining meringue buttercream around side of cake. Mark design on side of cake and make runout 80 below and frosted flowers, following step-by-step instructions on page 58. When dry, fix runouts and flowers to cake.

EXPERT ADVICE

≈

A ginger-flavoured meringue buttercream would be particularly delicious on this cake. Follow recipe on page 24 for Quick Meringue Frosting. When meringue is stiff, remove from heat and gradually whisk 2 tbsp ginger syrup (from a jar of stem/preserved ginger) in a slow steady stream. When incorporated and meringue is stiff again, gradually fold into softened butter.

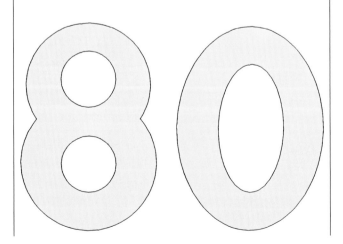

~ 1 ~

Smooth buttercream around the side by placing cake on a turntable or upturned cake tin. Hold a cake scraper or palette knife at an angle of 45° to the side of the cake and rotate cake with other hand until a complete circuit has been made. Repeat with a serrated scraper or use a fork to mark a vertical design, working from base to top.

~ 2 ~

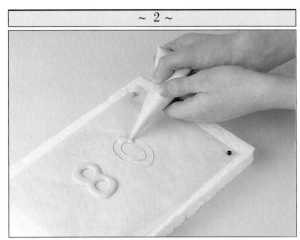

To make runout numerals, trace the 8 and the 0 on page 56, making several copies of each on the same piece of paper. Secure tracing paper to a flat surface with wax paper on top. Pipe outlines with coloured chocolate. Set for 1 minute, then fill in, moving bag to and fro. Use a cocktail stick (toothpick) to tease chocolate into corners.

~ 3 ~

Spread flowers for frosting on absorbent kitchen paper. Leave for 30 minutes, then shake gently upside down to dislodge any insects. Swish leaves through cold water, shake and dry on absorbent kitchen paper. Beat egg white lightly with 1 tbsp water. Brush all over front and back of each petal/leaf and down into any crevices.

~ 4 ~

Lightly sprinkle flowers/leaves with caster (superfine) sugar, gently shaking off any excess. Spread flowers out on wax paper. When dry, they will be firm and brittle and may be stored for a few days in tissue paper in a cardboard box. Always frost twice as many flowers or leaves as needed as some will not dry properly.

Garden Trug, see page 60

GARDEN TRUG

Illustrated on previous page

*A*lthough this cake uses the same basic shape as for Noah's Ark on page 46, the effect is quite different.

Quick Mix Sponge mixture, see page 8
Marmalade Glaze, see page 14
2 quantities Basic Buttercream, see page 18
juice of 1 orange
D E C O R A T I O N
750g (1½ lb) white marzipan (almond paste),
see Expert Advice
125g (4 oz/4 squares) dark dessert chocolate
(German dark chocolate)
yellow, green, orange, red and brown food
colouring

● Preheat oven to 180°C (350°F/Gas 4). Bake sponge cake in a lined and greased 20 x 30cm (8 x 12 in) cake tin (pan). Cool on a wire rack. Make several paper piping bags, following the instructions on page 34.

● Cut cake as shown for Noah's Ark, see step 1, page 46. Brush sections with marmalade glaze. Make up one quantity of the buttercream and stir in the orange juice to slacken. Using buttercream, layer the main sponge pieces for the trug. Leave to set for 30 minutes.

● Finish making trug and mould the marzipan (almond paste) vegetables, following step-by-step instructions opposite. When trug is complete and icing is dry, arrange moulded vegetables on top as shown in the illustration on page 59.

EXPERT ADVICE

≈

To whiten marzipan for cauliflower, knead in some food grade whitening powder, available from specialist cake decorating shops.

~ 1 ~

Having cut and assembled cake as for ark on page 46, trim front and back to make trug shape. Use trimmed wedge-shaped pieces to build up top edge of trug, positioning them at same angle as before, but reversing them. Roll 125g (4 oz) marzipan to a sausage; fit round top of trug. Melt chocolate; pour over top of cake.

~ 4 ~

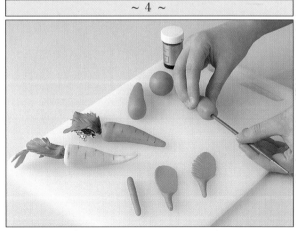

CARROTS AND PARSNIPS *Colour marzipan (almond paste), allowing 30g (1 oz) for each carrot/parsnip and 15g (½ oz) for leaves. Mould main pieces to 6.5cm (2½ in) cones. Mould each green piece into two 5cm (2 in) thin rolls. Flatten out at one end and snip down each side to feather. Push thin ends into vegetable tops; brush vegetables with brown food colouring.*

~ 2 ~

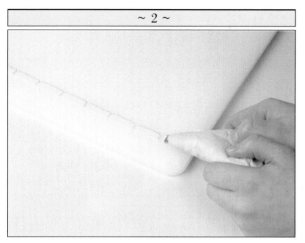

Coat ark thinly with buttercream. Put some buttercream in a piping bag with a basket tube (tip). Spoon a smaller amount of buttercream into another bag, with a plain no. 2 writing tube (tip). Pipe a row of ribbon strips, each 2.5cm (1 in) long, horizontally along the top edge of one side of trug, leaving a small gap between each.

~ 3 ~

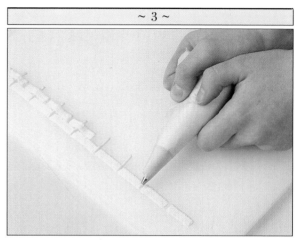

Using bag with writing tube (tip) pipe a line down between each ribbon strip to a point where a second line of ribbon would end. Pipe another row of ribbon, this time starting in the middle just below the first one. Pipe over first vertical line and end under the middle of the next ribbon, brick-wall fashion. Continue to build up pattern.

~ 5 ~

TOMATOES AND RADISHES Colour some marzipan, allowing 30g (1 oz) for two tomatoes or four radishes and 15g (½ oz) for radish leaves. You will also need a pea-sized piece of green marzipan for the calyxes. Roll main pieces into balls. Cut a star for each calyx and push into tomato. Make radish leaves as for carrots.

~ 6 ~

CAULIFLOWER Allow 30g (1 oz) marzipan for head; colour 15g (½ oz) green for leaves. Roll plain marzipan to a ball; mark floret pattern with skewer. Roll green marzipan into pea-sized balls of varying sizes. Roll out thinly between plastic wrap. Using small leaves first, wrap around florets, slightly overlapping. Smooth.

RASPBERRY VALENTINE CAKE

*F*resh raspberries are used to flavour this special occasion cake, but other soft fruits would be equally acceptable.

6-egg Genoese Sponge mixture, see page 10
125g (4 oz/1 cup) pistachio nuts, finely chopped
ICING
4 tbsp Sugar Syrup, see page 24
125g (4 oz/¼ lb) fresh raspberries, sieved into a purée
1 quantity American Parfait, see page 22
1 quantity Glacé Icing, see page 26
30g (1 oz) marzipan (almond paste)
pink food colouring
icing (confectioners') sugar for rolling out

❖ Preheat oven to 180°C (350°F/Gas 4). Bake cake in two heart-shaped tins (pans). Cool on a wire rack. Make several paper piping bags, following instructions on page 34.

❖ Warm sugar syrup and pour it into a small bowl. Gradually stir in raspberry purée, then chill mixture until it is thick enough to just coat the back of the spoon. Make up parfait in a large bowl. Set aside 1 tbsp of the thickened raspberry purée for piping; gradually beat the rest into the parfait.

❖ Using one third of the parfait, sandwich cakes together and then spread the rest around the side of the cake, bringing it well up to the top edge to form a little ridge. Press the pistachio nuts over the side of the cake.

❖ Following the step-by-step instructions on page 64, ice the top of the cake and decorate with marzipan hearts.

EXPERT ADVICE

≈

The feathering technique used for this cake may be adapted for cakes of all shapes and sizes. Concentric circles, dragged out from the centre in alternate directions, look good on a round cake. On a square cake, the circles may be piped to radiate out from one side. When dragged, a fan effect is created.

~ 1 ~

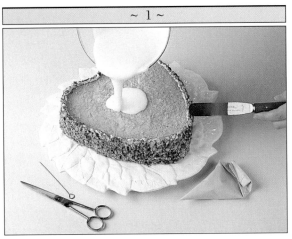

Put reserved raspberry purée in a piping bag. Have ready a skewer and a pin. Make up the glacé icing and immediately pour it onto the cake, starting in the centre and working towards the edge. The icing should flow over the cake. Use the skewer to tease it into any awkward corners. Prick any air bubbles with the pin.

~ 2 ~

Snip the point off the piping bag containing the raspberry purée. Pipe straight lines diagonally across the cake, 1cm (½ in) apart. If unsure about the technique to use, see page 50. The glacé icing should still be so soft that the purée sinks into it.

~ 3 ~

Quickly pull the top of the skewer across the cake, through the coloured lines. Make a second drag line 1cm (½ in) from the first, but in the opposite direction. Continue until feather pattern is complete as shown on page 63. See also Expert Advice, page 62.

~ 4 ~

Colour the marzipan pink. Roll it out on a surface lightly dusted with icing (confectioners') sugar to about 5mm (¼ in) thick. Cut out about 24 tiny hearts, using an aspic cutter, if you have one. Alternatively, make larger hearts, using a heart-shaped biscuit (cookie) cutter. Position hearts round rim of cake.

Christening Cake, see page 66

CHRISTENING CAKE

Illustrated on previous page

A basic Madeira, transformed to a light fruit cake by the addition of raisins, mixed peel, ground almonds and mixed spice, makes an ideal Christening cake. The basic cake and icing are suitable for a girl or boy; simply change the colour and motifs. To adapt the design, see step 6 opposite.

6-egg Madeira Cake mixture, see page 12
½ tsp mixed spice
125g (4 oz/ ⅔ cup) raisins
125g (4 oz/1 cup) mixed chopped peel
60g (2 oz/½ cup) ground almonds
I C I N G
1 quantity Buttercream Paste, see page 20
pink and green food colouring
almond essence (extract)
1 quantity American Parfait, see page 22
Apricot Glaze, see page 14

Preheat oven to 160°C (325°F/Gas 3). Grease and line a 20cm (8 in) square cake tin (pan). Make up cake mixture, sifting spice in with flour and folding raisins, peel and ground almonds in at the end. Mix to a soft dropping consistency, level in the tin (pan) and bake for 1¾-2 hours. Cool in tin. Prepare several paper piping bags, fitting one with a writing tube (tip) and snipping end of another to a 'V' shape, see page 34.

Make up buttercream paste, kneading in one or two drops of pink food colouring with almond essence (extract) to taste. Place paste in a polythene bag. Make up parfait. Set aside 12 tbsp for piping and colour the rest pale pink, a shade or two lighter than the buttercream paste. Set aside 6 tbsp pink parfait for piping.

Invert cake on a cake board. Brush top with apricot glaze. Cover and decorate, following the step-by-step instructions opposite.

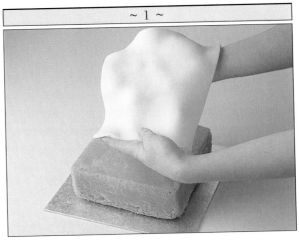

~ 1 ~

Having glazed cake, knead buttercream paste on a surface dusted with icing (confectioners') sugar. Roll it out thickly to a 20cm (8 in) square, using short, light movements. Run a knife around paste to loosen it, then slide hands underneath and lift it onto cake. Smooth gently with the palm of your hand.

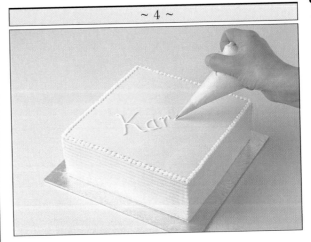

~ 4 ~

Write child's name boldly on a 20cm (8 in) square of greaseproof paper (parchment), place on cake and pinprick out word. Using piping bag with writing tube (tip) and white parfait, pipe name, using same technique as for straight lines, see page 50, but laying thread round to shape the letters neatly.

~ 2 ~

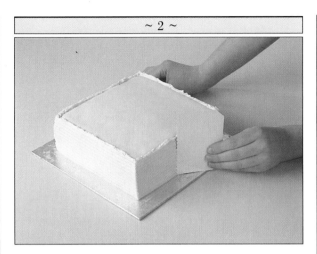

Spread parfait over sides of cake, working it up and down so that it comes well up to buttercream paste topping. Hold a serrated scraper at 45° angle to the cake. Starting at a corner away from you, quickly and firmly draw scraper towards you and up to a nearer corner in one movement. Clean scraper; repeat along remaining sides.

~ 3 ~

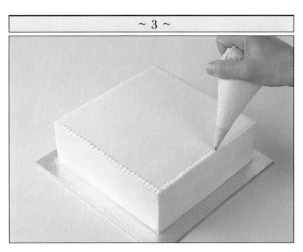

Place some reserved white parfait in a paper piping bag fitted with a small star tube (tip). Make border on top of cake. Holding tube at an angle of 90° to the cake, press out a little parfait to form a star. Remember to stop squeezing the bag before you lift the tube to make the next star, otherwise all the stars will finish in points.

~ 5 ~

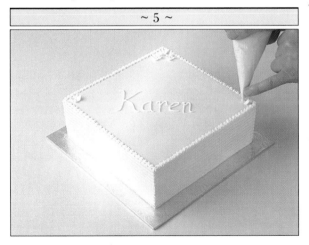

For flowers, fill piping bag cut to a 'V' end with white parfait. Place tube (tip) on cake, near a corner, and squeeze bag. Stop squeezing; sharply pull up tube at an angle of 45°. The parfait should form a raised petal. Pipe four more petals, then, with pink parfait, pipe centre. Pipe green leaves in same way.

~ 6 ~

Adapting design: For a boy, use blue buttercream paste and parfait. Trace teddy or similar motif and make a cardboard template. Make templates for each letter of child's name. Knead buttercream paste trimmings, roll out thickly; cut round teddy and letters with small knife. Lift shapes, brush backs with gin; position on cake. Smooth edges.

CHESTNUT CREAM LOG

*T*his may be served as an alternative to either Christmas pudding or the traditional rich cake.

2 quantities chocolate Swiss Roll mixture,
see page 10
FILLING
1 quantity Crème Diplomate, see page 16
250g (8 oz/1 cup) unsweetened chestnut purée
30g (1 oz/2 tbsp) icing (confectioners') sugar
2 tbsp rum
DECORATION
1 quantity American Frosting, see page 24
½ quantity American Parfait, coloured green,
see page 22
45g (1½ oz) marzipan (almond paste)

Preheat oven to 220°C (425°F/Gas 7). Bake both cakes in lined and greased 20 x 30cm (8 x 12 in) Swiss roll tins (jelly roll pans.) Roll up one of the chocolate cakes from the long side, see pages 10-11. Roll the other cake in the same way but over a rolling pin covered with greaseproof paper (parchment). Make several paper piping bags, see page 34.

Make up the crème diplomate. Beat the chestnut purée, sugar and rum together and fold into the crème. Fill and roll the log, following the step-by-step instructions opposite. Chill for 30 minutes, as directed, then refer to the step-by-step instructions on page 70 for frosting and decorating. Keep the finished cake in a cool place and eat within two days.

~ 1 ~

Carefully unroll the thinner Swiss (jelly) roll. Spread half the chestnut cream over it, spreading it with a palette knife. Roll the cake up again and hold it for a few seconds with the join underneath so that the shape sets. Spread roll with remaining chestnut cream.

~ 2 ~

Carefully unroll the Swiss (jelly) roll from around the rolling pin and wrap it around the first roll, tucking the join underneath. Wrap the cake in greaseproof paper (parchment) and place it in the refrigerator for 30 minutes to set. To decorate, see page 70.

~ 3 ~

Having filled and rolled log, see page 68, make American frosting. Unwrap log, place on cake board and cover quickly with frosting; cover length of log first, then ends. As icing sets, swirl it with a warm dry palette knife or mark woodgrain down the length with a fork.

~ 4 ~

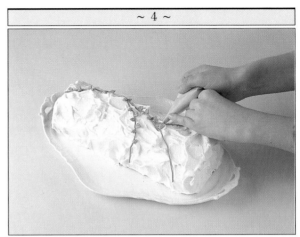

Place green parfait in a paper piping bag, snip off end and pipe ivy stems over the cake as shown on page 69. Fill a second bag with parfait; snip end to 'V' shape. With tip of bag on ivy stem, apply pressure with your little finger. Squeeze bag, drawing it sharply away to form a leaf. Make remaining leaves in the same way.

~ 5 ~

For trees, cut marzipan (almond paste) into three equal pieces. Mould each to a cone. Spoon green parfait into a piping bag fitted with a small ribbon tube (tip). Pipe small parfait ribbons around each cone, starting at the base. Bring tube sharply down and then sharply up and away from cone each time to break off parfait. Top each tree with an upright strand.

~ 6 ~

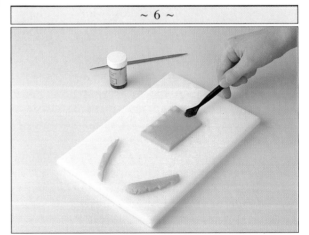

If liked, the remaining marzipan (almond paste) may be used to make a greetings card. Roll marzipan to a 5 x 7.5cm (2 x 3 in) rectangle and mark edges with fork or modelling tool. Pipe a greeting or design of leaves and berries, using the bag cut for piping the ivy stems. Alternatively, paint inscription with a fine paintbrush dipped in green food colouring.

GLOSSARY

BEAT/CREAM A technique for mixing soft ingredients, usually with the intention of incorporating air. Using a strong wrist action, a wooden spoon is pushed through the mixture in a circular movement, trapping air when lifted. An electric mixer may be used.

BLEND To gently mix ingredients together, either by stirring or by *folding in*, see below. Also used for processing ingredients in a blender.

CHILL To cool food, either in the refrigerator or in a cool larder. Hot ingredients may be chilled quickly by placing the container in a bowl of ice cold water or ice cubes.

COAT To cover cakes with an outer coating of glaze, cream, icing or melted chocolate.

CREAM See Beat.

FOLD IN To incorporate an ingredient into a lighter one without knocking out the air, as when sugar is added to whisked egg white. A large metal spoon is cut through the light mixture, which is then lifted up and folded over the heavier ingredient, using a figure-of-eight action. Care must be taken to scrape and lift the mixture from the base of the bowl, and to prevent the heavier ingredient from sinking and settling. Mixing should stop as soon as the heavier ingredient has been incorporated.

FONDANT Traditional fondant icing is made by boiling sugar and then working the syrup into a paste. It is then warmed and thinned to be poured over cakes. Do not confuse with sugarpaste, which is sometimes referred to as fondant icing.

FROSTING A cooked or partially cooked icing, originally comprising egg white and sugar syrup. Today more usually applied to a variety of cooked icings that can be smoothed or swirled and which dry to a crisp surface while remaining soft underneath. See also page 24.

GÂTEAU A light sponge cake sandwiched and decorated with a rich light filling of cream, meringue, fruit or enriched icing.

GENOESE A light sponge, enriched by melted butter, made by the whisking method.

GLAZE Literally 'to make shiny'. In sugarcraft the term is used when melted jam or jelly is applied to a cake to seal it and add flavour.

GREASE To brush a tin (pan) or lining paper with melted vegetable fat (shortening) or oil to prevent ingredients sticking when cooked.

KNEAD This usually refers to heavy beating of a dough, but when used in connection with marzipan or icings, only a light pressure, applied by the fingertips, is required. The mixture is pulled out at one side and stretched before being pushed back on top of the main piece. The mixture is worked until smooth and pliable.

NOZZLE See Tube.

SIEVE A metal or nylon mesh utensil through which soft food is pushed in order to create a purée. Also used for dry ingredients such as flour, when the intention is to remove any lumps.

SIFT To shake dry ingredients through a sieve or sifter to combine them, to reduce the size of grains and to incorporate air. Ingredients should be sifted in small batches.

SLACKEN To make a substance - often a batter or icing - less stiff, usually by adding a liquid.

SYRUP A sticky solution made by boiling sugar. Used to enrich icings, soften chocolate and thicken fruit purées.

TUBE (TIP) One of a range of small metal cones, each with a shaped aperture at one end. Placed at the end of a piping bag, it shapes the icing as it is forced through it. Also known as a nozzle.

INDEX

FOR FURTHER INFORMATION

Merehurst is the leading publisher of cake decorating books and has an excellent range of titles to suit all levels. Please send for our free catalogue, stating the title of this book:-

United Kingdom
Marketing Department
Merehurst Ltd.
Ferry House
51-57 Lacy Road
London SW15 1PR
Tel: 081 780 1177
Fax: 081 780 1714

U.S.A.
Sterling Publishing Co. Inc.
387 Park Avenue South
New York
NY 10016-8810, USA
Tel: (1) 212 532 7160
Fax: (1) 212 213 2495

Australia
J.B. Fairfax Press Pty. Ltd.
80 McLachlan Avenue
Rushcutters Bay
NSW 2011
Tel: (61) 2 361 6366
Fax: (61) 2 360 6262

Other Territories
For further information contact:
International Sales Department at United Kingdom address.